Assessment

A practical guide for primary teachers

Margaret Sangster and Lyn Overall

p. 1
p. 28
p. 144.
p. 151.

continuum
LONDON • NEW YORK

Continuum
The Tower Building
11 York Road
London
SE1 7NX

15 East 26th Street
New York
NY 10010

www.continuumbooks.com

© Margaret Sangster and Lyn Overall 2006

British Library Cataloguing-in-Publication Data
A catalogue record for this book is available from the British Library.

ISBN 0-8264-8463-8 (paperback)

Typeset by Ben Cracknell Studios
Printed and bound in Great Britain by MPG Books Ltd, Bodmin, Cornwall

Also available from Continuum:

Howard Tanner and Sonia Jones: *Assessment: A Practical Guide for Secondary Teachers*

Also by the same authors:

Margaret Sangster and Lyn Overall: *Primary Teacher's Handbook*

Margaret Sangster and Lyn Overall: *Secondary Teacher's Handbook*

Contents

List of figures

List of tables

Acknowledgement

We have many people to thank for the help they have given in writing this book, especially the many teachers, trainees, teaching assistants and children who have willingly offered their stories. In particular, our thanks go to the head teacher, and all the staff, both teaching and non-teaching, and the children and their parents and carers at Owler Brook Nursery Infant School, Sheffield, for the privilege of allowing us to share some of their excellent practice with you.

Introduction

Assessment exists to promote learning and to inform others about what has been successfully learned. As Gipps and Stobart (1997, introduction) put it, 'Good teaching is about motivating and helping children to learn.' They go on to add, 'Teachers typically treat assessment as a necessary chore rather than an intrinsic part of the process.' This book is about practical steps in making assessment a central activity for teachers, a part of the process rather than an 'add on'.

We have three principal sources of inspiration. It has been our privilege to work with many, many talented teachers who, apparently effortlessly, know so much about the learning processes of the children they work with. It is clear that for them, teaching, learning and assessment have to be considered together. This book is about why this is an effective way to teach and how you can make this happen in your classroom. Seeing them work with pupils often in challenging settings, has provided the strategies, ideas and illustrations for many of the actions we suggest.

In England publications such as *Inside the Black Box: Raising standards through classroom assessment* (Black and Wiliam,1998) have influenced many researchers and writers (Clarke, 2001, 2003; Torrance and Pryor, 1998). These publications and subsequent conversations with university colleagues and school inspectors are another important source for our thinking about classroom assessment. In particular, we would draw your attention to the annotated list at the end of this introduction in which we recommend some further reading.

Work with trainee teachers and teaching assistants has been a third rich source. Trainee teachers on a variety of routes into teaching work hard to become at ease with the range and variety of activities that make up a teacher's role. Often, assessment is seen as an additional chore by them too. This can be a barrier to meeting the standards required to become a teacher. Helping students to make good use of classroom assessment on taught modules and by working with the teachers who mentor them on placement has also become a source for many of the suggestions we make. Teaching assistants' insight into the needs of the individual children in the class are often very illuminating. They get to know the children so well that they are able to make accurate judgements and predictions. The stories they tell have provided the basis for many of the examples we have used in the book.

Guide to the book

The first three chapters provide a general overview about the place of assessment in schooling. In Chapter 1 we remind you about the need for accountability and the way this is managed in England. Chapter 2 identifies the types of assessment that are used in classrooms, describing differences and the ways they are used. Chapter 3 takes you through the assessment that a child may face through his or her time in school, from assessment at entry, through the formal reporting stages at seven, eleven and fourteen with a brief description of public examinations at entry points to further or higher education or employment. At the end of the chapter a case study describes one nursery infant school's approach to teaching learning and assessment.

In Chapter 4 the approaches which are used by teachers and other adults to learning and assessment are compared and contrasted. Using the analysis of approaches used by teachers, Chapter 5 considers the implications these have for effective assessment. These five chapters form a background to the management of assessment in the classroom.

Chapters 6, 7, 8, 9 and 10 are about creating the opportunities to assess. In Chapter 6 the daily opportunities to collect and use data to inform teaching plans are explored. Finding the time to enable assessment to be central is described in Chapter 7. Chapter 8 is about involving children in their learning and assessment, how they can be encouraged to make decisions about their own learning, to form judgements about their successes and weaknesses and begin to think about the ways in which they learn. Chapter 9 explains how formative assessment is conducted through the moment-by-moment conversations that take place in classrooms. We explore the initiating questions, the answers, the probes, pauses and other techniques that get pupils thinking about what and how they are learning. Chapter 10 is about feedback, the ways in which children begin to understand their learning by what we say, and how we say it, both face to face and in writing.

The final chapter (Chapter 11) considers the teacher's recording of data and the recording of data by the child and the ways in which this, too, can be part of the process rather than an add on. The chapter deals with the ways in which records can be used by those who need information: with pupils, parents and carers and others both within and beyond the school. We illustrate this with a case study on assessment for pupils with barriers to learning.

Further reading

This book is about practical ways in which assessment is central to teaching and learning. The books below are particularly recommended as further reading.

Black, P., Harrison, C., Lee, C., Marshall, B. and Wiliam, D. (2003) *Assessment for Learning: Putting it into practice*, Maidenhead: Open University Press.

A two-year project with teachers gives this book its particular importance. What teachers say about the ways in which their practice changes as they place assessment in the centre of their teaching is inspirational.

Clarke, S. (2001) *Unlocking Formative Assessment*, London: Hodder and Stoughton.

Clarke, S. (2003) *Enriching Feedback in the Primary Classroom*, London, Hodder and Stoughton.

Down-to-earth, practical advice again.

Gipps, C. and Stobart, G. (1997) *Assessment: a teacher's guide to the issues*, London: Hodder and Stoughton.

A summary of traditional assessment methods used in education.

Hall, K. and Burke, W.M. (2003) *Making Formative Assessment Work: Effective practice in the primary classroom*, Maidenhead: Open University Press.

An excellent general introduction to making everyone a part of the assessment agenda, this book has particular strength in formative assessment in early years.

Torrance, H. and Pryor, J. (1998) *Investigating Formative Assessment*, Maidenhead: Open University Press.

Using extensive video and audio tape recordings of assessment in real classrooms which were then explored in interviews with teacher and pupils gives this book an authentic feel. Early years' settings provide many of the illustrations included.

Note on terminology

Vocabulary choice in this book includes 'children', 'pupils' and 'students' used interchangeably. We have used 'he or she' but on occasions, to make the text easier to understand, we have not used this convention. Likewise where the teacher in the example was female we have used 'she' and where male, 'he'.

1 Assessment and its purposes

Introduction

This opening chapter examines the role of assessment in the primary school. The nature of assessment as seen by others and the approaches used in this book are discussed. Assessment is viewed in the context of those who use its outcomes. We explore the tension created between the teacher who is using assessment to promote learning and other agencies who want a statistical snapshot of how children are performing.

Assessment is a process

Assessment is a process. Data are collected about a situation. They are then analysed and the results of the analysis are usually reported to someone and then used. Alternatively, the results can be acted upon straightaway. In education assessment has many purposes and many levels. It can be a comment from the teacher designed to help a pupil move on. This quick and informal exchange is as much part of assessment as sitting a three-hour public examination. In England in recent years, there has been much imposed, formal assessment, the results of which have been reported very publicly. Assessment has become closely tied to the idea of accountability. This has meant that some of the informal and formative aspects related to pupil learning have been left out of the definition and consequently been underused in the classroom. It is possible to argue that formative assessment has never been strongly part of traditional assessment methods and it is only in recent times, through the work of Black and his co-workers (see for example, Black, Harrison, Lee, Marshall and Wiliam, 2003), that it has come to be seen as significant. Either way, formative assessment is an important part of the equation in successful pupil learning. Clarke (2001, p.5) refocuses us when she comments, 'It is by good teaching and learning that standards rise, not by summative or short-term measures to boost attainment'.

Accountability

This word accountability encompasses a widely diverse set of expectations. Usually, schools worldwide operate in a climate of accountability. In the English education system, information about pupil performance is legitimately required by a number of bodies, who may need the same information presented in different ways, or, sometimes, even different information. Some of these bodies are both powerful and demanding; a teacher must respond to their requirements. Accountability is important if children are to get a fair deal and these requirements must be met. At the same time we cannot assume that assessment for these purposes provides information that is either sufficient or effective for good pupil progress. At best, they contribute to the picture of a school or pupil at a particular moment. These summative assessment are driven by and structured for purposes other than that of creating an assessment about an individual child's learning.

Layers of accountability

There are many layers of accountability, rather like an onion, with the teacher and the child at the centre from where interactions and events are broadcast outwards to various audiences. The immediate layer is to the teacher. Results of the effectiveness of the lesson are fed into the future planning and the progress in learning. Beyond this, the teacher reports to parents or carers, the head teacher, and subject co-ordinators. The next layer of the onion is the reports to the governors who need to monitor how well the school is progressing academically. This, too, is the concern of the Office for Standards in Education (Ofsted) and the Local Education Authority (LEA). The general public is also entitled to know how well a school is educating its youngsters. Finally, the government requires information about the education system to inform policy and to compare progress with other countries. All this seems a long way from one child's learning within the classroom.

The School Improvement Agenda

In England, the government is looking for evidence of school improvement. To provide this they choose a set of measures and then compare them with previous evidence against the same measures. When GCSE (General Certificate of Secondary Education) results are published, comparisons are made with previous years' results. What happens after publication is a debate about standards. One side, usually lead by the Secretary of State for Education, will make statements along the lines of, 'If more people pass then standards must be rising.' The other side will counter this success with the argument that tests are becoming easier and standards are really falling. Comments will be sought from employers: 'They may have GCSE Maths at grade C but they can't do the sums needed for my firm. What I need is someone who can learn new things quickly and effectively. New workers have to know how to fit in.' Older people will claim: 'education isn't as good as it was in my day'. This political football gets kicked around every year. This means that the students who have done the work feel their success has been devalued and the teachers, parents and carers feel uncertain about the status of the national exam system.

Whether standards are rising or falling what is important is to realize that expectations have changed dramatically. What was good enough in education even a few years ago would not give school leavers the knowledge, skill or attitudes they will need today. Increasingly there are very few jobs for people with poor literacy and numeracy skills. Tomorrow who knows what will be required. Educational reform (see information for England on www.teachernet.gov.uk/educationoverview/briefing/current strategy/) is beginning to respond to this. With proposed changes it is likely that there will be ways of measuring and valuing different types of progress.

Uses of data collected for accountability

Everyone wants to know 'which are the good schools'. Each school has a unique set of circumstances which means that the education it offers will have subtle differences from the school down the road. One school might serve an area where children come to school, as it were, 'test ready'. The school down the road may work with children who do not have this readiness, they have to learn 'how to do the test' from school staff. Pupils in both schools will make progress but one school will still appear to be better than the other because their children are already better at doing tests. In both schools, too, staff will work hard at improving measures of success which will enhance the profile of the school; they may offer a good sports or arts profile to attract new pupils.

Public expectations

The public is looking for a set of test results which show that pupils perform well at this school compared with the one down the road. This might be a problem for a head teacher who knows that the catchments of the two schools are widely different and her school is unlikely to do better than the other school in public test results. She will endeavour to improve the test results which might be based on a narrow band of academic achievement but may also choose to set up other measures of success which will enhance the profile of the school in the eyes of the public.

A school for a child; the parents' or carers' choice

Parents and carers want sound data to inform the choices they make for their children. Part of the information will be national test results. These show that pupils perform well at school x compared with the school y down the road. What else makes parents and carers choose one school over another? Generally they want their children to be happy, to have a 'good education', 'to learn useful skills', 'to do sport' or 'art' or 'music'. The wish list seems to be a mixture of the child's needs in social, emotional and intellectual growth. Clearly, school test results provide only a part of this information. It is reasonable to link school exam performance to their child's chance of exam success. It is more difficult to measure happiness. This is the kind of informal assessment which is passed by word of mouth within the community. As adults, this is an important factor in our life, so why not for children too? The reality is, that in the end, most children go to the nearest school.

Teachers and other school staff

Teachers are as concerned about good schools as the next person, in fact more so, as it this is their profession. They do not want to work in a school that has a poor reputation. They do not mind working in school where the work is hard because the children present particular challenges. This reasoning applies to the other staff who work in schools as well, teaching assistants, office staff, cleaners, all want their school to have a reputation of doing well for the children. In schools where it is tough, staff want these barriers to learning to be recognized and reported in the debate on national test results. The measures that teaching staff take to meet all the needs are found in their School Improvement Plan. This is where they outline how they intend to meet the targets they have set for themselves or those set by outside bodies such as the local authority and Ofsted.

With all the demands of public accountability it could be easy to view pupils as those who generate the statistics; it is easy to be lured into thinking that setting higher goals will motivate children to achieve. This may not be so. It might be an incentive for raising achievement and to raise parents and public expectations but in the centre of the onion are the pupils and the teacher who are engaged in the practical task of education. This is the prime task, not externally driven policies.

The teacher seeks to educate the child. However, in the primary school where they are with the children nearly all the time, their educational goals go beyond ensuring academic progress. They are also committed to ensuring that each child becomes a good member of the class, kind and thoughtful to others, self regulating in their own behaviour, hard working, able to celebrate success and deal with failure. They want children to be like this around the school, in assemblies, the playground and the dining room. They are also concerned that children learn many more things than maths and English. They realize that to narrow their teaching down to these two subjects will not necessarily lead to educational success. Success for pupils comes through a subtle interplay between subjects and children's confidence and internal needs.

The local authority view

The local authority wants all its schools to be successful. Success for them is measured by results and the improvement year on year of those results. They do look for 'value added' as well. These data mean putting some context to the results explaining how barriers to learning are dealt with. Some LEAs set schools targets based on the results of the baseline assessments. These are usually negotiated with senior school staff.

A school might have 47 five-year-olds of whom:

- 10 children have achieved all the Early Learning Goals (ELG);
- 30 children are working on Step 3 ELG;
- 7 children are still working at a lower level.

The targets set, based entirely on maths and English performance, would be, at the end of Key Stage 1, for these same children:

- 15 children who achieve level three;

- 32 children who achieve level two.

If this is the only measure of success then it is not sufficient. As you can see, it is measuring the success of a school on a narrow academic curriculum. It misses the point by underselling what good education is about. For some schools it takes a great deal of time and careful teaching to get children to be able to do the things that managing the learning for thirty children as a class requires. In school things such as 'sit and listen', play reasonably with others, hold a pencil, finish tasks are alien ideas to some children. It may take these children a great deal of time to be ready to do well at what they are tested on, the maths and English. In such a school, staff may need to be very good at getting children to feel confident and be successful in a range of things before they are able to help them make progress in maths and English. The targets set are not a true record of the progress made with many children.

Ofsted's approach

Ofsted (Office for Standards in Education) does take account of academic results but also concerns itself with the way schools operate and the quality of the teachers and school environment. These broader criteria are reflected in the reports which they publish for every school they visit. You can see what Ofsted inspectors look for in their reports by going to www.ofsted.gov. uk/reports.

To summarize, the easiest, but perhaps the laziest, way to compare schools is to use national test results. This gives a crude guide to standards. It is, nevertheless, still a legitimate way of measuring the education within a school. The danger is to see this as the only way of measuring a quality education. School staff are in the business of producing good citizens who will contribute to society in a number of ways. One impact of the focus on narrow academic achievement is that there is, inevitability, a long tail of pupils who fail. Some children never catch up; their test results, despite best efforts, remain at best disappointing, at worst a disaster. We are left with the question, are we measuring the things we value for children to be successful in society?

The impact of national tests

In England the amount of assessment required to meet the needs from beyond the classroom has created a huge workload. This has squeezed the time spent on the most productive form of assessment, formative. We are just beginning to rediscover the power of integrating formative assessment into a teaching model which ensures pupils have an opportunity to respond to their own performance.

With all the demands of public accountability, it could be easy to view pupils as those who generate the statistics and it is easy to be lured into thinking that setting higher goals will motivate children to achieve. Far from it. It might motivate schools to achieve and raise parents' and public expectations but in the centre of the onion are the pupils and the teacher who are engaged in the practical task of education.

The teacher's role and assessment

The teacher's concerns will be to meet a variety of needs. There will be the need to meet the demands of outside agencies with their requirements for snapshots of progress, but there will also be a need to have an ongoing model of assessment which feeds into the learning process. This model should also encompass both the assessment of the teacher's progress in providing effective lessons and the assessment of individual pupils' progress. One might describe these two needs as summative and formative assessment. The first summarizes a situation and is the 'snapshot' of what pupils know. The other, the formative model, informs us about what the pupil knows and what action should be taken. These are familiar terms in educational assessment and one assumes they operate within the system, but do they? Summative assessment is easier to achieve because there is no follow up. Formative assessment, to be truly formative, needs to have a response time and it is possible that this is difficult to achieve within current classroom practice.

Pupils' inner needs and assessment

Pupils are concerned with achieving goals that meet either their inner needs or those set by others. Meeting either inner motivational needs or those that are externally driven is a big factor in their progress. Summative assessment results, such as GCSE or Key Stage 2 national tests may well be effective external influences. If children do well then they will continue to work hard for similar exams, wanting to do the work right and to good standard because this makes them feel proud and good about themselves and aligns with an inner need. Little is made of inner needs in some classroom practice. This is a pity because when children work to meet their inner needs they will sustain effort over time to achieve goals. They will work hard and they will celebrate when they have achieved. If children in the class get to be able to do this for at least some of the time then the learning that goes on in class is going to be so much better. It is here that formative assessment has a role to play with daily feedback seen as an opportunity to improve one's own performance.

Summary

In this chapter we have reviewed the tensions that arise from the accountability regime established for English schools. The need for an accurate picture of any school's academic perform-ance is not disputed. The goal of raising standards through publishing the results in a narrow range of subjects has had some unexpected consequences. The league tables, which are sup-posed to assist parents in making choices, as well as driving up standards, have not been particularly helpful. The narrow focus on maths and English means that the richness of experience that can be offered to children is not easy to capture. In many schools the shift of the assessment focus to something that happens at fixed points has meant that the moment-by-moment formative assessment has been seen as a less important classroom activity. We argue that feedback, formative assessment to pupils, is a central teaching role.

Assessment can become an effective part of the teaching cycle which operates within the primary classroom. This includes not only assessment of pupils but also the assessment of effective teaching. Assessment will be viewed as a process which can be applied to many situations and the types of assessment are just the tools that you use to gather the data to inform your practice. For too long assessment has been seen as something that can be attached to the rest of teaching: almost as an optional after-thought. Recent work by Black *et al.* (2003) indicates that formative assessment has a much bigger role to play in learning. Torrance and Pryor (1998, p.20) consider 'classroom assessment is a social construction, accomplished by teachers and pupils through social and pedagogic interaction'. This makes formative assessment central. For this to function effectively, fundamental changes might need to occur in the way we approach our teaching.

2 Assessment types

Introduction

When assessing, the teacher's concerns will be to meet various purposes. There will be the need to meet the demands of outside agencies with their requirements for snapshots of progress, but there will also be a need to have an ongoing model of assessment which feeds into the learning process. This model will need to encompass both the teacher's progress in providing effective lessons and provide feedback on individual pupils' progress. The first summarizes a situation and is the 'snapshot' of what pupils know, this is summative assessment. The second is formative assessment because it informs us about what the pupil knows and what action should be taken. These are familiar terms in educational assessment and one assumes they operate within the system, but do they? Summative assessment is easier to achieve because there is no follow up. Formative assessment, to be truly formative, needs to have a response time and it is possible that this is difficult to achieve within current classroom practice. There are many terms used when describing types of assessment. Here we consider four types which will be referred to in the book.

Summative

Summative assessment can be likened to taking a snapshot of a situation. Information is collected and analysed. Examples of summative assessment are end of topic tests, end of year exams, GCSE exams, end of year reports and spelling tests. They tend to come at the end of a set of work. Often they are tests of memory and measure how much pupils know. They are more useful when they test what pupils know and can do, tests of application such as a problem to solve. Whatever form they are presented in, there is no follow up on successes and failures. The result stands as a signpost along the road of educational achievement. Contrast this example:

> In the classroom it might be that you need to know how well the class has understood the science topic. This is needed to inform you about how effective your teaching has been. This will also indicate how much the pupils have remembered. You may need to know this to enter it against National Curriculum targets; therefore you need to collect data about individuals. You may set a written test. Some questions will be about the terminology and some will be about situations so that they apply their knowledge.

With this:

> In the classroom you want to know if they have remembered what they learned in a geography project. You may need this information to see if your teaching has been generally effective. You are not particularly concerned about individual performance this time but would like it to be a review of the topic; therefore you decide to set a quiz which they will do in teams of four.

In these two examples the style of the assessment is driven by what you wish to know and do with the data collected.

Formative

In many respects formative assessment takes similar forms to summative assessment. The ways of collecting data will be similar. It is the intention that is different. The intention of formative assessment is to act upon the results. It is only formative if some action is taken. Formative assessment currently has a broader remit than summative assessment. The minute-by-minute interactions between teachers and pupils and between pupils themselves can also be defined as formative because the same process takes place. Here are ways that formative assessment makes an impact on what the teacher provides and what children are doing.

You need to know if the pupils understand what you are teaching them over the next three days.

Day 1 To find out about this you use question and answer periods during the whole-class teaching. You also set tasks to consolidate understanding and talk to individuals whilst they work on the tasks. You will ask lots of, 'Tell me what you have done', and 'Can you explain?' questions during the individual work.

Day 2 The pupils complete a worksheet on time. You collect these and mark them. The marking gives you information about what's known and what's not.

Day 3 The next day you select two key questions which several pupils got wrong and go through them with the whole class. You then give 10 minutes' paired work to discuss other errors or work on a supplementary task.

Diagnostic

Sometimes detailed information is needed about a focused area of knowledge. Maybe a child is struggling or everything seems too easy. The teacher then sets out to collect in-depth data so that he or she can address issues. As action will be taken it is also formative assessment. Diagnostic assessment can be time-consuming. It is used when there is a barrier to learning. So far we have suggested that pupils will achieve their learning targets without too much difficulty. If you have used your knowledge to work with them on tasks that match their needs and guided them through the learning then the endpoint assessment should give good results. They will know the material and be able to use what they know in their work. However, there will always be some children who find some learning troublesome. What should we do about this? Sometimes some children just need more time, more examples and slightly more guidance from you. Sometimes we need to find out more about what it is that is holding up learning. This is where we think diagnostic assessment approaches can be helpful.

> Peter's phonic knowledge seemed less secure than others' in the class, so over a week's teaching his teacher made a point of consciously noting which sounds he used to work out words when reading. She collected this information as part of her routine teaching. Reviewing her list of his phonic knowledge, she then checked this over with him by playing a series of sound bingo games, phonic snap and by having him read some target words.

Notice that the diagnostic approach checks what Peter knows in a variety of ways. The importance of phonic knowledge for anyone is to be able to use it in working out whether the word being read is 'bit' or 'bite', confirming that it was 'a bit of a do' rather than a 'a bite of do'. Her original observation was confirmed. Peter, at this point, does know fewer sounds than she would have expected and, furthermore, makes less use of the sounds he knows when reading new words.

What to do next? Peter, who is just coming up to seven years old, is making good progress in maths and other subjects. With this knowledge about his ability, the teacher decides that she needs to know whether the apparently poor phonic knowledge is making it difficult for him to learn to read. She collects some more information. She wants to know more about Peter so first she asks the expert, his mother. Peter's mother is the one who brings him to school, which means that the teacher sees her each day and they know and trust each other. She makes a time to talk with Peter's Mum.

> The conversation is friendly and the teacher takes great care not to alarm Peter's mother. Because this conversation is about a possible difficulty in learning to read she has two areas of particular interest, Peter's health and his interest in reading at home. Mum reports that Peter goes with her to the library every two weeks, 'he likes Thomas the Tank Engine'; she also says that he has had a lot of really bad colds since he started school, 'at least one every six weeks' but that recently he had seemed to be much better. The teacher explains why she is interested. While they talk she is evaluating the information. The interest in books that his mother mentioned confirms what she knows about Peter; she, too, has found him very ready to pick up a book. The bad colds during his school career to date probably mean that Peter has not been able to hear as well as he might, so he may have missed out on some phonics teaching. It is difficult to hear the differences between sounds when full of cold.
>
> In discussion it is suggested that Peter's hearing should be tested; although neither of them expects this to be a problem, it is agreed as a sensible precaution. The teacher asks for permission to use some reading tests with Peter. This is agreed. A time is set to review the information being collected.
>
> At this point they talk to Peter; again the intention is not to create alarm, but to keep him informed. He is used to having discussions about his learning with his teachers, so regards this as slightly more than routine, but nothing too much. They explain what is going to happen.
>
> During the next week the teacher and mother carry through the plan. The teacher selects a suitable reading test,

being careful to follow the instructions for the test; Peter enjoys the one-to-one experience with his teacher. Mother takes Peter to the doctor's where his hearing is tested.

The teacher and Peter's mother meet as agreed. The teacher by this time has gathered all the information she can on Peter including his reading from the time he joined school. Mother reports that the hearing test shows that Peter's hearing is fine. The teacher says that the reading test indicates that Peter is slightly behind what might be expected from boys of the same age. She also reports that during the week Peter has been doing extra work on his sounds. She thinks that this is beginning to work, that he is making progress in using phonics in his reading. The teacher and Peter's mother agree that they will meet in a month's time to see whether any further action is needed.

In this case, the teacher's knowledge about the reading process is secure. She knows how most children become literate. She is aware of the need for some phonic knowledge in the process of unlocking words. She knows what the children are expected to have learned at this point in their schooling. For this teacher this would also be true about the other subjects she teaches, for core curriculum listening and speaking and writing and for mathematics and science and for the other school subjects. She has a range of diagnostic approaches at hand. She is alert and looking out for children who may not be quite as far forward as she would expect. She expects to take time over Peter and any other child in her class who may need it. She is decisive; she acts to check on her observations, but she does not to jump to conclusions. She is respectful of the parents' or carers' knowledge and interest in their own children. She has built a reputation with them of being trustworthy and approachable. She thinks it important to work with the child and parents or carers and colleagues to avoid future problems. Her plans are thorough and thoughtful, fully part of her teaching. In this story the teacher worked within her own authority. Had Peter been less likely to make satisfactory progress, she would have worked with her colleagues to devise a teaching, learning and assessment plan, an individual education plan (IEP) to meet his needs.

To summarize, the diagnostic approach has the following features:

- observations based on knowledge and experience;

- alertness to possible mismatch between expected and actual learning;

- a range of approaches to check the child's learning;

- involving the child and the parents or carers in appropriate informative, helpful decision-making;

- effective time management to achieve sufficient knowledge to inform and carry out teaching plans;

- knowing when to seek assistance from colleagues in school.

Ipsative

Ipsative assessment is when progress is judged against previous performance. The judgement is tailored to an individual's achievements, as Torrance and Pryor (1998, p.36) put it, 'whether what they were doing now represented real progress for that child'. This is another type of formative assessment. If you believe that children construct knowledge best when it is based on and linked to previous knowledge then ipsative assessment will form an important part of your teaching cycle. Concept maps, where children identify what they know and what they need to know next, would be a good illustration of a response to ipsative assessment.

As part of the introduction, Year 6 children are asked to draw a concept map on their knowledge of fractions. They are asked to write down in a spider diagram what they know and what they think need to know about fractions. The topic is then planned, using the concept maps and taught. As a final activity the pupils return to the concept map to identify their own progress.

Journals are another example of this approach:

Pupils have reflective journals in which they write about their own progress in science. As part of the journal they are asked to reflect on their own understanding and set targets to improve their own understanding. Time is given during the week for them to work at their targets.

Here the children work together:

Time is given to pupils to respond to written feedback in their English work. They have to discuss with a partner how they might improve their work and then write a small extract which addresses the advice given in the marking.

Some further examples of how these types of formative assessments might look in the classroom are given in Table 2.1 with an indication of the intended audience.

Table 2.1 Examples of assessments, the type and the audience

Assessment	Formative/ summative	Audience
Spelling test	formative/summative depending on whether re-tested	pupil/teacher/parents or carers (because they are probably expected to learn them at home)
GCSE (16+ national tests)	summative	pupil/parents or carers/ government/public
Individual discussion of work in progress	formative	pupil/teacher
End of topic test	summative (possibly formative if the topic is to be revisited)	pupil/teacher

Table 2.1 continued

Assessment	Formative/ summative	Audience
Individuals set own targets	ipsative	pupil/teacher
Worksheet as part of learning	formative	pupil/teacher
Teacher interviews on one-to-one basis and sets tasks to meet a need	diagnostic	pupil/teacher
Tables test	formative/summative depending on whether re-tested	pupil/teacher/parents or carers (because they are probably expected to learn them at home)
National tests (at 7, 11 and 14)	summative	pupils/parents or carers/ school staff (individual results) LEA/government/ public (statistical results)
QCA optional tests (in between national tests' years)	formative	teacher/pupil/school (to inform teacher/school of progress towards national tests and practise exam conditions)
Concept map (individuals identitify known and unknown)	ipsative	pupils/teacher
Question and answer in class	formative	pupil/teacher

Summary

As a teacher it is important to decide for what purpose you are collecting information and what information would best tell you what you need to know. This will then help you decide how best to collect that information. Assessment should always have a purpose. The information you choose to collect and the information you choose to record should always be used to inform someone and the information should be revealing.

Some useful questions to ask are:

1. Why is the information needed?
2. Who needs the information?
3. What information would best serve that purpose?
4. What is the best way to collect it?
5. What are the data telling me?
6. What aspects do I need to record?
7. How can I respond to this information?

Gipps and Stobart (1997) state that assessment should fit the type of data to be collected or the action required. If the teacher wants learning of facts, then testing might be an appropriate strategy. They warn that more complex activities may not be possible to assess simply. This is a trap that many assessment systems fall into. When the first national tests were introduced they tried to measure complex situations such as problem-solving. History shows that this was time-consuming and difficult to judge and the national testing system quickly moved to a much more simplistic model. The trap is to assume that tests such as the national tests measure the complexity of skills and knowledge owned by each child. They are simply a snapshot of a limited set of knowledge in a narrow range of subjects. It is important that teachers and schools promote the educational achievements of the whole child, not only to others but to the children themselves.

3 Assessment through the year

Introduction

This chapter considers the assessment journey that children experience through an academic year. When a school is visited for a short period of time it is hard to see the whole assessment picture. Here, the kinds of assessment that pupils experience and teachers use are discussed. Some of these are official requirements; others are normal assessment practices. There are many bodies requiring information about the children in your class. Assessment practices described range from informal lesson-by-lesson processes to the national examination experience, from subject review through to report writing for parents. Both formative and summative assessment have a part to play. The 'assessment journey' as outlined here includes what happens and when, through the years of schooling in England, where assessment is currently the most prolific. The description is based on a three-term year. Some minor adjustments will be needed if you work in a school that operates a four- or six-term year.

Tests and examinations

National testing is a dominant feature of the English education system. When very young children enter school an assessment will be carried out to find out about aspects of their development. These are used to plan teaching and learning for each child's

progress. You can find out about this assessment by going to
www.qca.org.uk and clicking on 'foundation stage'. It should
be stressed that these are not tests but they establish a starting
place for later measures of progress. From the age of seven many
children will be in a regime of regular testing. The tests at age
seven are to continue the monitoring of progress. Later national
tests are used to make statements about achievement. Many
schools like to keep the summative testing routine going by
providing optional tests at the end of each year. Regular
summative assessments bring with them messages of expectation
of achievement throughout a child's time at school. As you will
see in Table 3.1 some of these tests are mandatory. These are
produced by the Qualifications and Curriculum Authority
(QCA). You can find out about these tests by going to www.qca.
org.uk and clicking on 'tests'.

The other tests that schools use may be standardized tests from
organizations such as the National Foundation for Educational
Research (NFER). Again if you go to www.nfer.ac.uk and click
on 'tests and assessment' you can find out more about these.
Standardized tests try to measure how an individual at a particular
chronological age compares against a whole population, a five-
year-old against all five-year-olds, and a thirteen-year-old against
all thirteen-year-olds. They provide a means of comparing one
five-year-old against many five-year-olds; thirteen-year-olds'
performance in science in one school with thirteen-year-
olds' performance in science in many schools. They can be used
to compare groups in various locations. These are tests which
have been trialled and, when used with care, can provide sound
data. Table 3.1 summarizes the testing and examination experience a child in England might expect throughout their schooling.

This picture changes from time to time. For seven-year-olds
there has been a shift from universal testing in favour of a
preference for ongoing profiles. Policies do change and develop
as teachers feed back concerns and issues to bodies such as the
QCA. If teachers act as co-policy-makers, then they need to take

Table 3.1 Assessment from entry to leaving school in England

School stage	Assessment	Age
Entering the foundation stage	Informal collection of baseline information	3/4 years
Leaving the foundation stage	Foundation Stage Profile	5 years
End of Key Stage 1	National Curriculum Tests	7 years
During Key Stage 2	e.g. QCA optional tests	8/9/10 years
End of Key Stage 2	National Curriculum Tests	11 years
During Key Stage 3	e.g. subject tests set by school teachers	12,13 years
End of Key Stage 3	National Curriculum Tests	14 years
End of Key Stage 4	e.g. GCSE	16 years
Key Stage 5	e.g. GCSE, AS levels,	17 years
Further study	e.g. A levels, GCSE/VCE	18 years

every opportunity to voice their views. Thoughtful and evidence-based responses to requests from official bodies from teachers can make a difference to the daily work in the classroom.

As the curriculum in English secondary schools has changed and is changing to accommodate the complex needs of pupils, from the age of fourteen the national qualification framework applies. Pupils at this stage can opt for a mixture of general, vocational and occupational awards. This has meant that as well as more choice, there is more testing as well. At sixteen the traditional academic route is to take the General Certificate of Secondary Education (GCSE) followed by, at eighteen, GCSE advanced level. There has been an increase in testing with the introduction of AS levels, which come between GCSE ordinary and GCSE advanced level. The Advanced Subsidiary (AS) is a stand-alone qualification and is valued as half a full A level qualification. The A2 is the second half of a full A level qualification. In September 2000 the advanced GNVQ was replaced by the vocational A level Vocational Certificate of Education (VCE). You can find out more about these changes on www.qca.org.uk/ and by going to the 14–19 home page.

Assessment through the year

Interwoven between these official points are all the assessments which take place from day to day and from term to term and year to year. For every teacher, each year has an assessment shape to it. Whether you are taking over a class in September or doing a teaching practice in a school you will need to gather initial information so that you can pitch the work at the right level from the beginning of your contact with the pupils. This preparation will include beginning to form working relationships with the children, finding out what they like, what they are good at and the targets and expectations that they have. See the case study at the end of this chapter where we tell the story as it is in one nursery infant school.

Table 3.2 Terms and assessment points

Autumn Term

Weeks 1–5	Introductory phase: forming relationships, establishing class routines
	Reviewing knowledge
	Introducing new learning
Weeks 2–3	Preparation for parents' or carers' first meeting
Week 4	First parents' or carers' meeting
Week 5	Outline of new learning for children and their parents and carers
	Half-term review:
	Formative assessment in maths and English
	Summative assessments in other subjects

Weeks 5–12	Learning, teaching and formative assessment
Week 13	End of term review:
	Formative assessment in maths and English
	Summative assessments in other subjects
	Interim report to parents or carers (optional)
	Parents' or carers' meeting (optional)

Spring Term

Week 1	Introductory phase: reviewing routines, knowledge, introducing new learning
	Outline of new learning for children and their parents and carers
Weeks 1–5	Learning, teaching and formative assessment
Week 6	Half-term review:
	Formative assessment in maths and English
	Summative assessments in other subjects
	Target setting with children
	Interim report to parents or carers (optional)
	Parents' or carers' meeting (optional)
	Outline of new learning for children and their parents and carers
Weeks 7–12	Learning, teaching and formative assessment
Weeks 12/13	End of term review:
	Formative assessment in maths and English
	Summative assessments in other subjects
	Interim report to parents or carers (optional)
	Parents' or carers' meeting (optional)

Summer Term

Week 1	Introductory phase: reviewing routines, knowledge, introducing new learning
	Outline of new learning for children and their parents and carers
Weeks 1–5	Learning, teaching and formative assessment

Week 6	Half-term review:
	Formative assessment in maths and English
	Summative assessments in other subjects
	Target setting with children
	Interim report to parents or carers
	Parents' or carers' meeting (optional)
	Outline of new learning for children and their parents and carers
Weeks 7–12	Learning, teaching and formative assessment
	Preparing the children to transfer
Weeks 12/13	End of term review:
	Formative and summative assessment in maths and English
	Summative assessments in other subjects
	Final written report to parents or carers
	Parents' or carers' meeting
	Final review and target setting with each child

Introductory information

The first person requiring information about pupils will be the class teacher who is going to teach the class in September. Many teachers will pass on information to the teacher inheriting their class in two ways: formally, though written records, and informally. Much useful data are exchanged verbally in the staff room and at handover meetings. At such meetings it is possible to acquire knowledge on class dynamics, friendship groups and barriers to learning as well as academic ability. To make transition from one class to another as easy as possible, it is likely that teachers will swap classes in the weeks before this happens. There will be written information to aid this process. If you are a student or trainee you will need to acquire similar information.

If children are changing schools, these meetings are more difficult to organize. Ideally, the children will have met their new teacher in the familiar setting of the class they are used to and will visit the new school on at least one occasion before they move up. Some schools have a well-developed system for smoothing the path from infants to juniors and juniors to secondary. These will often involve pupils from the receiving school acting as buddies and mentoring new children through the routines they will need to know. To ensure that the transition is managed, information is presented more formally and in writing. The new class teacher will probably inherit record cards and brief notes about the academic performance of each child plus any particular barriers to learning which need to remain on record.

This information gives the new class teacher a good start in organizing the classroom and planning the level of the work. However, children change over the summer and work differently for different teachers so the first few weeks will be a time of getting to know the class by collecting lots more information. This will be a delicate balance between providing new work and checking up on knowledge already held. Lessons will have a flavour of review and move-on and the teacher will be recording observations to create his/her own picture of the learner.

The daily formative process

This review process will merge into the daily formative process of planning, teaching, gathering information about learning and planning new work in the light of your findings (see Chapter 6). As information builds there may be some children you become concerned about who previously have not been noted as requiring additional support. The ongoing records that you keep will help to support your case when you seek additional help. You may be required to make a summative report for the SENCO (Special Needs Co-ordinator) or outside agencies. You will draw upon your knowledge of the child and your ongoing records of progress to compile this report. In infant and nursery schools many parents and carers collect their children from school. This provides an opportunity for informal discussion and issues can be resolved quickly before the need develops for more formal measures. This helps to reduce anxiety for all concerned.

First meeting with parents or carers

Some schools will have an early parents' and carers' meeting to inform them about how well their child has settled into their new class or new school. The content of the meeting will be an exchange of information between parents and teacher about the well-being and initial progress of the child. The formative records will inform your comments. Listening carefully to parents' and carers' opinions and views will add to your under-standing about each child.

In infant and nursery schools this first meeting often takes place prior to the child attending school. The teacher will make a visit to the child and parent or carer in a familiar setting, the child's home. This serves two purposes: it brings the parent or carer and teacher together in the child's eyes and, the child meets the teacher on their own territory and can show them his or her things, like best toys. By giving the child this experience the school visits can be more successfully managed. For the teacher it helps to make sense of some of the reasons behind children's responses when they enter the classroom or nursery.

The half-term review

Within the National Numeracy Strategy (DfES, 1999) two days each half-term are blocked out in the medium-term plans for assessment and review. You might use these to provide a formal test of the knowledge retained by the pupils from the half-term's work. The National Numeracy Strategy (NNS) indicates that it is a time when the teacher reviews work with pupils he/she is not sure about, focusing on a group and tasks which will cover the area where pupils may or may not have grasped a concept. This implies that the teacher is focusing on only a few pupils at this point and really updating their formative records. This could be seen as a formative process because there is a spiral curriculum in the NNS and the main topics are revisited in the following half-term. This means that use can be made of the information gathered. English also provides opportunities to revisit skills and knowledge, probably more frequently even than mathematics.

For other subjects this may not be so. In geography and history a topic may only be visited once in the primary school. An assessment of the topic is likely therefore to be summative. However, there are skills which are reapplied in both these subjects so they may form the basis of a formative assessment. Checking thing like 'Can they use an index in the atlas?' are worth tracking. So are things like placing an event on a time line, planning a route on a map and identifying the main factors influencing a historical event. These are all skills and processes we would expect children to acquire on a more permanent basis and be able to use again and again.

End of term

End of term assessments are often similar to half-term strategies. You will have collected and recorded information to show individuals' progress against learning objectives. This will be used to report to pupils, to parents or carers and will accumulate to provide a progress report for the whole year. There may be another parents' meeting where the emphasis will have moved to the teacher reporting on each child's progress and identifying areas where he or she needs support at school and at home.

End of year

Again, there will usually be a parents' and carers' meeting in the final term. This will review the child's progress using mainly summative assessment. One aspect of this meeting may be to set tasks for the summer holidays related to target setting. The emphasis of this parents' or carers' meeting should be about the celebration of achievement. Some schools link the event to an exhibition or a performance. Some schools invite the children to bring their parents and act as a guide through the school. In some ways, the guided tour is a reversal of the home visit. Here we see the child at home in the school environment and empowered to conduct their parents around an alien environment. It is worth noting that best practice is for issues that concern individual children to be dealt with, by appointment, at another time.

The end of year will bring more formal tests for some children. National testing tends to be scheduled for May and June with results coming later in July and August. Some schools conduct optional tests purchased from organizations such as QCA and NFER. These are seen as summative and formative, indicators of future performance in national tests and as exam practice. The results are usually reported to parents and carers, either at a meeting or in a school report.

In England, legally, a written report must be provided each academic year. Very often this an end of year report. In Reception classes, two reports are sometimes provided, one 'settling in' report in the first term and one end of year report. The style of report varies considerably. All will contain official national tests results and all report on the National Curriculum subjects which the child has studied. Beyond this, the extent and nature of the comments is up to the policy of individual schools. You will find different practices:

- a selection of phrases;

- tick boxes;

- written comments;

- or a mixture of the above.

Usually the author is the teacher, countersigned by the head. But some reports have contributions from the children. Each school decides the emphasis and detail of the report. Target setting is sometimes included although this is very difficult to follow up at the end of the year. (Further reference to report writing can be found in Chapter 11.)

Transfer

Finally, the teacher will be expected to pass on information to the next teacher. There is always a dilemma about what information should be sent on and whether it is used. This has particularly been the case when pupils change schools. If the school does not have a procedure in place then individual teachers decide what to 'send on'. Our view is the minimum it would be helpful for the next teacher to know about is:

- the level of performance in each subject (which may include test results);

- aspects of learning that show strength;

- aspect of learning which need to be worked upon;

- particular interests;

- any particular requirements or barriers to learning (e.g. something physical like poor hearing);

- attitude to work;

- ability to work with groups;

- independence and autonomy;

- self-discipline and regulation.

It is often useful to report on social, emotional and moral development as well. This might include comment on or reference to:

- friendships;

- ability to handle conflict;

- attitude to school.

Whatever is reported, comments need to be brief and informative but fair. There has to be evidence to support the comments. The report should be positive. Negative comment may prejudice the next teacher's opinion. At the same time, however, the information must be honest. The aim of any reporting is to ensure that the transition is smooth and the pupil has an opportunity to make a good start with their new teacher. There is a case to be made for the ownership of any records being the pupils. This is something that is at present unusual. It is worth considering whether or not the pupil should know what the teacher has said about him or her.

Case study: managing assessment in a nursery infant school

As an illustration of how the above might work in practice, a case study has been included. It is about assessment policy operating in a nursery infant school. This case study is not a work of fiction. It does, however, take aspects of 'best practice' from more than one setting.

The approach to assessment

Each session is seen as an opportunity to let children discover more about their learning. There is a recognition that the curriculum needs to be covered but also real attempts to meet the needs of each child as well. As the head teacher said, 'A good lesson is defined as each child knowing more, building on new learning. The method [we use] is talking and listening to children whilst they are working, it is not about the marking. Each lesson should add a little bit to each child's knowledge, understanding, thinking and happiness. Children need to take the lead in their own learning.'

Developing the approach

An opportunity was taken when the school moved into the new building a few years ago to review all the practices that staff had developed over the years. This meant that some things that teachers and teaching assistants had been doing for years, well-ingrained habits, were really carefully thought about. As you may imagine, this was at times a painful process but, as staff were in broad agreement that 'Children need to take a lead in their own learning', ways of working were found to bring this about. Making the change was tough going. It was difficult to leave what was familiar and go on a new journey. Two teaching staff did leave during this time of change. But most stuck with it. In the beginning developing the policy for assessment was time-consuming because staff realized that, by putting the child's needs at the centre of the process, every aspect of their teaching had to be thought about. If learning is central then the teacher's ways of working have to become more guidance approach than control approach. While working on assessment they took the opportunity to review all aspects of teaching and learning. Keeping the child's needs central is now established through the school.

The formal process to keep the policy up to date and in everyone's daily way of work is an annual review of the policies. In the weekly planning meetings this aspect of teaching is planned for, assessment has to meet the needs of the age group as well. Also this school has all sorts of visitors so almost every week you will hear a child, a teacher, or teaching assistant explaining what it is they are doing. And, of course, every time a new teacher and new trainees arrive, they get a thorough briefing as well.

This is the way policy is worked through. Nursery staff will think about the needs of the youngest children, what needs to be assessed and how. They will develop their ideas by presenting their assessment plan to the Reception staff. This sharing helps Reception staff to understand their colleague's procedures and recording. Reception staff have their own ideas and will make suggestions. When Nursery and Reception staff are happy with their plans these are presented to a whole-staff meeting so that everyone has a clear idea about the assessment of children in the Nursery. All the year group teams use the same process:

- develop an assessment plan suitable for the age group;

- share with colleagues who teach the year group below and the year group above;

- then share with all staff.

This means that adjustments for each year group can be made. On the broad agenda the policy takes account of the need to report as part of the national picture, including inspection, dealing with children who have special needs, and reporting to parents and carers. The importance of partnership with parents and carers is high in this school, their views are thought of as extremely valuable in planning learning for children.

Recording assessment in the classroom

The assessment on each child is shared with that child all the time and, very deliberately, with the child's parents or carers. This starts in the Nursery where children will begin to be taught ways of telling teachers about their learning. Throughout their time in school these very young children work with teachers and teaching assistants to begin to understand what and how they are learning. They gradually become used to asking and answering questions that probe their own knowledge and understanding and ask about how they learn. They become used to this being recorded. In the Nursery the recording is on their own card, something which each child is proud of; they regularly show 'my card' to all visitors and, of course, to whoever picks them up at the end of the session. As the children worked on colour mixing the teaching assistant will encourage them to talk about the way they are working and what they have learned. At the end of the task this is what might happen:

> TA: Did you enjoy that?
> Gus, Ali, other children: general noises saying basically 'yes'.
> TA: Should we put it on your card?
> Children: Yes.
> TA: What was it we did?
> Gus, Ali and the rest supply a variety of answers and add their own questions.
> The TA supports this, gradually reviewing with them what they have learned, then with each child briefly writing a few words to record the task outcomes for that child.

By the end of their time in Nursery most children can tell you, with considerable confidence, what they like and what their best work is. They have begun to develop a way of talking and thinking about their own learning.

Nursery to Reception transition is carefully managed with Nursery children attending sessions in Reception, as visitors, until they are used to the new routines. At the transition from Nursery to Reception in a one-to-one conversation each child picks three things they want to do in Reception into their new workbook.

Once in school a new workbook is given out to each child every five weeks. The children do all their recorded work for the core curriculum in this book. Each child's workbooks are retained by the school as an important part of the evidence base for tracking progress. The Reception teacher has the Nursery record as well. From these two sources of information she is able to plan the first five-week broadly based outline block of work which meets the needs of the children.

The half-term review

In Reception six children are reviewing with their teacher the learning they have done over the last five weeks and setting some targets. They are seated in a group. Each child has a conversation with the teacher while the others work individually. She encourages the child to work through his or her book pointing out to her things that he or she liked, work that he or she did well. Because all the written work for maths, English and science is in one book this is a straightforward process. The teacher will also ask each child about other learning experiences, reminding and reviewing with them oral language use, physical skills, mental maths, the things that are enjoyed and those which are not. The teacher or the teaching assistant will have recently completed a reading record with the child, hearing him or her read while noting miscues and approaches to unknown words, level of understanding and enjoyment of the text. At the end of this section of the review the child is asked to say which was the best piece of work and which was best liked. The review then moves on to target setting. Targets are recorded in a new workbook. These children are new to Reception so the teacher only asks for one or two targets. Often, at this stage, the children will want to target things like handwriting and tidiness. The teacher has to work with each child, encouraging them to think about learning. Targets may include getting better at particular processes, 'explaining how I get the answers to my sums', or doing more, 'I'll write three sentences every day', or something general, 'I'll listen to the instructions more carefully before starting my work.' Some of the children are confident writers so these children will be encouraged to record for themselves. For others the teacher does the writing. Five weeks later these same children will be reviewing their progress against these targets. You can imagine that by the time children are in Year 2, at seven years old, they are pretty good at knowing what they know and how they learn best. Many of them can hold their own in discussion with each other and with adults, use reasoning to come to decisions, and realize that what they decide will have an effect on others. This has to be a promising start as lifelong learners.

Reporting to parents and carers

The relationship between school staff, parents or carers and particular children starts long before the formal entry to Nursery. Home visits are thought of as a central plank in ensuring that there is openness and clarity about the child and his or her needs. Many parents and carers in this community have had little to do with schooling. If they were born here their experience of school may have left them with at best neutral views about teachers, at worst hostility. If they are recent arrivals to the area then they will be anxious about any authority figures. School staff have had and continue to have considerable amounts of training in preparation for home visits; the raising of awareness about different cultural practices continues to be very important. Successful visits leave everyone feeling more confident, the child, the parents or carers and others at home, and the teacher.

The crèche and community teaching room are a useful bridge into the Nursery. Contact can be built up at the pace that suits the family. Very gradual extensions of time for some children on their introduction to Nursery can be a great help. Before this facility was built children came to Nursery for the length of time they could manage until they could settle in for a full session.

Once in school the teachers are systematic in their use of informal feedback to parents. The recording system of the card in Nursery and the workbook in school make this straightforward. As most children are collected at the end of the school day by a parent or carer, during each half-term each teacher makes sure that what the child is doing in the curriculum and learning progress is explained in very short but frequent meetings.

These informal meetings are supplemented by a variety of teacher, child, parent or carer events. These events include formal reporting on each child's progress when the written report can be explained and explored. Meetings are timed to suit the parents and carers. Some are during the school day, some before school and some immediately after school. If none of these times suit the parent or carer then a home visit may be arranged.

In all cases the written reports are shared documents: the child, his or her parents or carers are given clear, accurate information. The outcome of the meeting is intended to lead to action: things that teachers will do, things that the parents or carers will do and things that the child will do. In this multi-ethnic, multi-lingual school the child's written report may need to be translated. In some cases it may need to be read to the parents. This is where the bilingual teaching assistants are invaluable. School staff will, where necessary, call upon the services of translators from the community to ensure that needs are met.

As you can imagine in an area of ethic diversity and real poverty, links between home and school have to be worked for. In the beginning, several years ago, on the old site and in the old school, home visits before the child started school, with access to a toy library, were a first step to remove barriers between home and school. Providing a parents' classroom for English language teaching was another early move. Parents' classes, especially for the women in the community, have been an amazing success, starting from one a week several years ago, to now, in the new facility, two or three each day. Some of these are group meetings where parents, carers and others in the community discover how children learn particular topics. The deputy head runs regular drop-in sessions on infant maths, the Literacy co-ordinator does a similar series on aspects of reading, writing, listening and speaking and other co-ordinators run occasional sessions on their subjects. The community teacher who organizes this seems to be some sort of genius, her power to persuade the reluctant to join in is amazing. This is the children's policy in action and it is impressive.

All this is supplemented by the usual things that infant schools do to get parents and carers involved – e.g. every religious festival has its own celebration with every child in school taking part. Then there are the picnics, the parties, the garden, the book fairs – you name it, these children, school staff, parents and carers do it! The Leavers' Assembly shortly before the seven-year-olds finish in the infants is a high spot celebrating each child's achievement through the school. This is the one that the children really remember, with a bravura performance from the head teacher as the real highlight.

A school like this with its commitment to high standards is an exciting place. It challenges school staff to be the best. It is, as you can imagine, very hard work; it can be frustrating when things do not go to plan, when a child you thought would do well on national tests goes away for three months, when the co-operation you have worked so hard for breaks down, but, when it works, you can imagine how satisfying it is.

4 Learning and assessment: the teacher's role

Introduction

Learning for any of us is about long-lasting change, it is what we know and can do, our likes, dislikes, all those things that make us who we are. Our learning comes both from our genetic make-up and all the experiences we have: our home, community, race, culture and gender all play a part in our learning. This chapter is about how teachers and co-workers deal with learning. The understanding that adults have about learning is central to what happens with children in classrooms. To explore this, the chapter focuses on two approaches to learning which are modelled on the work of Louise Porter (see, for example, Porter, 2003, Chapter 2, 'Debates about Discipline'). The different approaches show how central the teacher's knowledge and beliefs about children and learning are. In one approach the teacher is very much in control of the learning; in the other the teacher's role is seen as informed guidance. Of course, both approaches have implications for assessment practice. We address these in Chapter 5 as well as, in depth, throughout the book.

In both the approaches it is assumed that the teacher's ability to teach the subjects is secure; that the teacher will have the accurate facts, clear concepts and procedures for teaching subjects. Thorough teaching will be measured by assessment at appropriate endpoints to find out what is known and understood and what the pupil's application of knowledge and understanding is. Even though the pupil will be in a class of thirty, both approaches assume a context in which each child is valued as an individual, that each child will learn in his or her own way and that this will be unique to the individual. Both approaches recognize that in any class there are likely to be groups of individuals who will have similar learning needs and can be taught together, as well as some very able children and some who will have either short- or long-term barriers to learning.

One important difference in the approaches is the relationship between teacher and pupil. In one approach the focus is on the teacher: the process of learning is teacher-centred, with the pupil almost as a passive recipient. This approach is about the control adults have over the child's life in the classroom. The second approach is centred on the pupils: it is their needs that have to be met. In this approach the adults take on a guidance role, the teacher assists the choices that are driven by the pupil. In the first approach the teacher is in control, he or she is the boss, in the second approach the teacher takes on the role of leader. Different ideas about inner needs and external control, goals, view of pupils, view of learning, adult's status and interventions in learning and conduct arise from the two approaches. The section below introduces each of these ideas and they are summarized in Table 4.1.

Inner needs and external control

In a control approach the teacher rewards or punishes the learning that the pupil undertakes. The pupils attempt to answer all the sums that have been set, the teacher rewards the right answers with ticks, praise, and possibly a sticker. The answers that are wrong are punished with crosses. The rewards are intended to help pupils to work hard to get the sums right and to avoid the mild punishment that follows when the answers or methods of working are not correct. This is the sort of common sense approach that has real appeal. The analogy that springs to mind is that of getting paid for the work we do: do the work and you get paid, cease to work and the money stops. In this approach the control is beyond the person being controlled. The pupil is controlled by the teacher and the wage earner by the wage provider.

In the guidance approach all the choices are worked out with the individual. The pupils choose to work out the answer to the sums because they want to. Maybe they gain intellectual satisfaction from the task. The tick or the cross for right or wrong answers is feedback on performance rather than reward or punishment. It is not that they are unaware of the reward, of course, as this is part of the classroom culture; rather it is that they really like doing sums. In a guidance approach, even if we have a big win on the lottery we might choose to continue to work because we 'enjoy it'. The locus of control is internal; people are meeting their inner needs through their own actions, by completing the learning task to their own satisfaction.

This can be illustrated by thinking about the child's view of learning in this story:

A group of five-year-olds has been set a maths task. They are asked to build a brick tower for each number on the work card. On the table are suitable bricks to make the tower and a set of stand-up number cards to show how many bricks are on each tower. For example, on the work card the target number might be two; to be correct, the child builds a two-brick tower and finds a stand-up number 2. The work is supervised by an adult who provides appropriate feedback: 'Well done, that's a two-brick tower and you've labelled it with a 2'. Three out of the four children quite happily get on with the task. Soon brick towers begin to appear all over the table. James, however, completely ignores the task; what he does is

to build the highest tower he can. He has subverted the task
set by the teacher. The teacher checks to see if he has
understood the task. He has; it is just that he has chosen not to
do it. He knows perfectly well that what he is doing may well
get him into trouble. He is prepared to take the risk of
punishment to do the self-chosen task.

Guidance theorists explain this story by pointing out that we are
all controlled from within. The distinction between children's
learning and performance goals has a part to play in our
understanding about learning. Children who want to learn as an
inner need are likely to be successful whichever approach we
use. If a guidance approach is used it is more likely that we can
move children who have performance goals to align learning to
meet their inner needs. (For more on this, see the Appendix
where a theory about motivation is described, Dweck, 1989.)
In a guidance approach, the feedback supplied by the adult in
providing information about success or failure on the number
task is designed to tell children what they are doing, to support
their internal needs. Contrast this approach to that when the
feedback is used to manipulate children's responses. If the adult
in the story rewards success in the learning task then this means
that the control is external. In a control approach the expected
outcome will be that all the children in the group will work to
gain the reward. However, even then, their willingness to
undertake the task cannot be attributed to the reward alone. It
is just as likely that they may have found the task one that
matched their internal needs; in this case exactly the same words
as are used to reward, or punish, will be used by the child as
guidance from the adult.

What, then, of James? In this story James decided, that for
him, it was worth the risk of not getting a reward, in order to
do what he wanted. What conclusion can we draw from this? If
we choose to use control as a principle we are likely to find our
efforts subverted. Even when punished, unco-operative children

are not likely to conform. Indeed, some will argue that this will make them even less likely to conform. Their internal needs take precedence: for them punishment, even the mildest like the withholding of reward, is not going to have the predicted effect of forcing them to conform by completing tasks. The more rewards and punishments that are used with unco-operative learners, the more likely it is that, instead of changing, their internal needs become more fixed. What seems, at first, to be common sense, is not such a good idea.

In the long term, working with pupils using guidance approaches is likely to have more mileage. Children are much more likely to learn well if there is a match between the task and their inner needs. If they are willing, they will do the task irrespective of reward or punishment. If they are not willing, like James in the story, then they will use the tasks for purposes the teacher did not intend.

Teachers' goals

Teachers' views about what schooling is for are going to determine how they act. If it is seen as about empowering children to become problem solvers and critical thinkers, then the guidance approach will prevail. If children are seen as John Watson saw them, then behaviourist methods will prevail. He wrote this:

> Give me a dozen healthy infants, well formed and in my own
> specified world, to bring them up and I'll guarantee to take
> any one at random and train him to become any type of
> specialist I might select – doctor, lawyer, artist, merchant, chief
> and, yes, even beggarman, thief – regardless of his talents,
> penchants, abilities, tendencies, abilities, vocations and race of
> his ancestors. (Watson, 1930, p.104)

In the control approach adults direct the learning that is to be done; in essence it is a behaviourist approach.

Postmodernism, which sees children as part of a complex ecological system, actively constructing their own experiences (Dahlberg *et al.*, 1999), moves the focus from adult-directed learning. If children are seen as curious, inquisitive and competent individuals who construct what they know and need to know, then the emphasis shifts. The adult listens and responds, and supports and encourages the individual in learning. This is a guidance approach; this comes from a social-constructivist view of learning.

The status of the teacher is different in the different approaches. Teachers who control use their authority to be the boss. They have the right to demand that children learn in ways that they have decided. The communication is likely to be: 'I ask the questions and the children provide the answers'. Teachers who use a guidance approach use their authority to lead. They see themselves as more experienced, more knowledgeable, but not more important than the children they work with. The communication in the guidance approach is likely to be more conversational, with the child sometimes taking the lead in the discussions about learning.

Teacher in control approach

This has some strengths. In this approach learners are recognized as individuals: it is realized that one pupil's knowledge, understanding and ability to apply what he or she knows and understands is not the same as any other pupil's. The teacher's role is to make sure that learning happens. Children are expected to comply with the learning that is offered. They are expected to learn in the ways that the teacher decides. Often, in this approach, the focus is on endpoint assessment. The teacher will test knowledge after a block of teaching has been delivered. Differentiation in the teaching will be based on how well, or badly, pupils do on the test. There are many teachers who are quite happy with this as a model. They would argue that it fulfils the role well.

Teacher as guide approach

In this approach, rather than putting the teacher at the centre, attention is shifted to the pupil. The guidance teacher takes a different view about teaching and learning. Learners are expected to be self-aware and self-reliant, to have a view about what they learn and how they learn. If pupils are at the centre, it is they who will be able to:

• forecast how well they will do on tasks;

• know what they understand about tasks;

• know what aspects of the task they can already do.

This means that the adults in the children's lives guide them towards being able to make these decisions and choices for themselves. To do this, at first, children will be asked: 'How well do you expect to be able to build and label the number towers?' Gradually the children will be expected to ask and answer this and the other questions for themselves. Furthermore, the pupils who can do this are more likely to be able to transfer what they know to completely new learning tasks. This is a key idea in lifelong learning. It has as a philosophy the need for each of us to be able to respond in flexible ways to the new challenges we face and will face throughout our lives. Modern societies need individuals who can take on new roles as they arise. This willingness to learn to do new things demands self-confidence and self-knowledge.

View of children

The views we hold about children make a huge difference to the approach that we adopt. Going back to the story, the teacher who uses a control approach will have a different interpretation about James to that of the teacher who uses a guidance approach. James is known to know his numbers, so the task should be one at which he can succeed. In the control approach, one view would be that he is being 'naughty'; he is defying the authority of the teacher. The teacher taking this view will see this as something that needs to be corrected. James will need to see the error of his ways and be 'ever so gently forced' to do the task to the teacher's satisfaction. This is because 'you can't let them get away with it'. You have to act to prevent further naughty, i.e. off-task, behaviour. Once again this seems a beguiling argument; children are a blank canvass, Watson's view, which adults have to paint. At the same time, most likely the teacher who acts like this believes, as most do, that education should be a positive, child-centred enterprise. Simultaneously, he or she is also holding and acting on a completely different and negative view about children being in need of correction. It very easy to send a mixed message to pupils.

However, in the story the teacher acts consistently using a guidance approach. Her leadership role shows considerable insight about James. She ignored James's initial response; in doing this she implicitly acknowledged his internal need to build the very tall tower of bricks. Later, she talked to him about the task and agreed to work with him so he could complete it, which is what happened; he did the task, explaining to her all about the numbers as he worked. A more controlling teacher would have taken a different approach, perhaps punishing James with a minor verbal rebuke, and insisting on the completion of the task then and there.

View of learning

The third difference between the two approaches is the view that the teacher takes about teaching and learning. At a general level, the control approach will favour what has to be taught over what the learner needs to learn. In the control approach the curriculum, rather than the needs of learner, is much more likely to be in the forefront. This can lead to wide coverage of content at the expense of understanding in depth. As the guidance approach is much more focused on the learner, the curriculum content may be of less concern. In the guidance approach the processes of learning are likely to be forefronted. If the teacher takes a controlling role, then there are at least three effects on learning. First, some children will come to rely on the teacher to tell them how to undertake tasks. The external control exercised by the teacher will have the effect of limiting children's abilities to become self-reliant and able to make decisions about how to work. This may mean that, when presented with choices about what to learn and how to learn, they become unable to make these decisions without considerable adult help. As it is too risky to make their own choices – 'you might be wrong and then you get punished' – these children may want to be told, at every point, exactly what to do and how to do it. Secondly, because the teacher provides the judgements about how well they perform on any task, rather than developing their own ways of learning and reflection, children become reliant on the external, probably summative assessment. Work becomes about getting ticks for right answers. This may well limit their ability to make sound judgements about the work that they do. Because they are not able to make an informed prediction this means that they do not really know what it is they know; nor are they sure about their learning processes. Thirdly, as the power seems to lie very much with the teacher, this may mean that children have difficulty in telling the teacher about what they know. As one child said to one of the authors, 'It is the teacher who tells you what to do, and how to do it, so don't *you* ask me, just you tell me what you want me to do.' There was no notion of partnership in this child's view of school learning. He clearly saw it as: you do as you are told, that is what teachers are for, to tell you what to do. This seems to miss the importance of school as a space where it is safe to learn the negotiating skills that adults need in everyday events at home, at work and in social life.

The guidance approach reverses these effects. Here the relationship between the teacher and the learners is somewhat different. First, the teacher will be encouraging learners to have an active say in how they may achieve in learning tasks. For this to be possible the teacher needs to be aware of the knowledge, concepts, skills and processes of the subject that the child is being asked to learn. The aware teacher will be very clear that subjects have some easy bits and some which are much harder to grasp, and which bits are which. The teacher knows those bits of subjects which are hard to learn. He or she will take extra care to guide children through the tricky bits, coaching and supporting them in their learning. One child showing one of the authors his poem, said about his teacher: 'I found this bit hard, I mean what rhymes with "bow"? Mr Jones, he sat with me and a few others and we just worked away at all the words we knew until I had enough to get the next line right.' In responding to what the pupil needed, the teacher used leadership and guidance to help.

Secondly, because the teacher takes time to develop reflection with the children, they will begin to have an informed opinion about how well they may do on any task. Over time this knowledge about learning develops until learners are usually accurate about it. This ability to know what you know and what you may need to know is immediately important in classroom learning.

Self-knowledge is a powerful tool in developing awareness about how learning works. This is a central idea in this book. Teachers will be guiding children in making predictive judgements. By asking 'how well will you do?', the scene is set for the question 'how well did you do?' and 'how are you going to do it?' and 'how well did that way of doing it work?' By building these steps into learning events, over time and with support, most children, even very young children, become really perceptive about their own learning. Because the children begin to be able to set themselves realistic targets, the teacher can more

Table 4:1 Summary of the differences between control and guidance approaches

Approach	Control	Guidance
Locus of control	External	Internal
Goals	Teachers make learning happen	Teachers guide learners so that they can: forecast how well they will do on tasks; know what they understand about tasks; know what aspects of the task they can already do.
View of learning	Focus is on curriculum delivery for all Teacher's judgement about progress Teacher decided how tasks are to undertaken Learners rely on teacher's rewards and punishments Teacher tells, learner does	Focus is on appropriate curriculum for individual learners Shared judgement about progress Learners have ideas about how they approach particular tasks Learners have some ideas about their success on tasks Learner has a say in what and how they will learn
View of children	Naughty	Will do the work if he/she sees the point of it Leader
Adult's status	Boss	Acknowledgement
Intervention methods	Rewards Punishment	Problem-solving

readily use a guidance approach. For children and adults it becomes all right to know that learning some things requires more effort, and reassuring to know that some things are going to be easy to learn. This awareness will be useful in adult life where predicting what will take effort and what will be easy is part of being a lifelong learner

Thirdly, with the guidance of the teacher, learners will be developing the vocabulary and concepts that let them have a conversation about progress, success and weaknesses on tasks. In the guidance approach phrases that may be heard when teachers are working with children include 'I think I'll be able to do. . .', 'I expect to do well because. . .', 'I'll need help with. . .', 'I'm going to try doing that by. . .'.

Summary

Whilst it is possible to recognize each teacher's general approach to learning as either control or guidance, there are many occasions when the predominant approach will be abandoned. In some contexts a teacher whose approach is usually that of leader, becomes the boss. Where it is necessary to prevent a child coming into danger this is easy to understand. The information must be correct, Eskimos do not live in igloos and they are not Eskimos but Inuit. Similarly, a process of subtraction that is not going, ever, to give a reliable answer needs to be diverted. However, our observations lead us to suspect that the shift in approach is entirely likely in any learning event. In the story about James, the adult involved may have well moved, seamlessly, from one approach to the other. For some children this will be confusing; they will learn better if the approach is consistent. But mostly children seem to deal with the ambiguities that adults in their lives have. It seems to be a feature of human beings that we can, at the same time, both hold and act on two contradictory views.

5 Learning and assessment: implications for assessment

Introduction

This chapter considers the implications for assessment of using either a guidance or control approach. Three areas are discussed: effects on open formative assessment, what is taught and teaching children how to learn. Whether teachers adopt a guidance or controlling approach, thorough teaching is required in both. How do you work out which approach you naturally use? What are your answers to these questions? When you begin to work on a new aspect of a subject, can the children in your class tell you:

- how well they think they will do on new work?

- what they already understand about the work?

- what they know about how it?

If they can, then they are in control of aspects of their own learning. This would suggest that you have adopted a guidance approach. If, instead, the answer is they cannot predict and need you to prompt them about what they already know, it is more likely that you are making these judgements for them. Perhaps this means that often the control approach is being used. Table 5.1 provides a summary that outlines how the two approaches impact on learning.

Table 5.1 What do teachers do to help learning?

A teacher's role as boss	A teacher's role as leader
1 Find out what the pupil knows, understands and can do	Help the pupil to find out what he or she knows, understands and can do
2 Decide on the next set of learning outcomes	Use curriculum knowledge to work with the pupil to decide on the next set of learning outcomes
3 Design a suitable teaching event to match the learning outcomes, sharing the learning outcomes with the pupil	Work with the pupil to design a suitable teaching event to match the learning outcomes, sharing the learning outcomes with the pupil
4 Teach, provide the pupil with knowledge, understanding and ways of using knowledge and understanding Find out what the pupil knows	Teach, provide the pupil with knowledge, understanding and ways of using knowledge and understanding Find out what the pupil knows
5 Repeats Step 3–4	Repeats Steps 1–5

You will note from the table that both approaches require effort and commitment from teachers. It is the impact on a child's ability to be an autonomous learner that is a key difference. In the guidance approach there are three ideas that underpin and help to create autonomous learning: formative assessment, thorough teaching and teaching children how to learn.

Before going any further, it is important to note that all the adults in a child's life in schools need shared values and knowledge as they will all have an impact on every child. As a teacher you will be taking a lead in establishing the approaches to teaching learning and assessment in your classrooms. You will have co-workers, teaching assistants, to support children's work. In one Infant school in England we recently counted six adults in the classroom. In addition to the teacher there were three teaching assistants and two placement students all working with children. To make best use of all these adults your philosophy, your views on teaching, learning and assessment have to be clear and carefully shared. In this school, time is found for this. Teachers, teaching assistants and trainees plan all their work together as co-workers in twice-weekly sessions, while the children in the class work with either the head teacher or the deputy head. In whole-staff meetings co-workers regularly discuss the approaches they will use to learning. This is excellent practice and works to the advantage of every aspect of classroom and school life.

Open formative assessment

In Chapters 1 and 2 the centrality of open formative assessment was discussed. As children come to our classrooms knowing many things about the way they learn, our job is to make use of this in our teaching. In a guidance approach, central to this is our ability to work with each child to monitor what he or she knows and understands about what they are learning. There are at least two aspects to this. We need to find ways of making clear what he or she knows and what still has to be learned. We also need to help children understand how it is they learn. This is the first key to using the child's internal needs to further his or her learning.

Rewards and feedback

Of course, all the children, willing or unwilling, need to know how they are doing; in the guidance model, rather than the feedback being about reward, it is about the success on the task. Assessment that provides information about the correct answer and ways of working is necessary. The comment on the effort the child makes, 'You worked hard at the task', can be used in either approach. It is the underlying message, the intention of the adult that needs to be understood. The same words used in the guidance approach is feedback, whilst in the controlling approach, it is reward. What, in the control method, are rewards and punishments, become part of the feedback strategies when used in the guidance model.

Using both approaches

We have already suggested that it possible, indeed inevitable, that you will use both approaches in your teaching. As many teachers will agree, it is much more satisfying for all concerned and much more productive for the children you will teach if you use a guidance approach. We expect that you will want to use the guidance approach as your predominant way of teaching. Our word of warning is that the guidance approach takes time to learn. One way to get started and build your own confidence is to start with subjects and topics that you are confident about and then work with a small number of children at a time. You can build up to all subjects, with all children all the time over the first few years of your career.

Is school-based learning different?

Another thing to think about is the differences between school learning and all the other settings in which children learn. The huge change for children entering school cannot be ignored. At home the child will, more often than not, both start and organize the learning. At home they ask the questions. In school, and at the classes and clubs that children attend, the control of learning moves away from the child. In these settings, even for very young children, play is often formalized and determined by adults. The adults ask the questions which the children are expected to answer. As children get older the curriculum will be increasingly dominated by what has to be learned and how it should be learned. Inevitably the locus of control moves from the child to the teacher.

Of course, it is true that teachers spend a considerable time thinking about how they can link home and school learning. When this is successful their classrooms often mirror the real world of the child. They recognize that children are often much happier if they are actively doing something. They know that many children prefer to make and do rather than sit and listen. The need to acknowledge some aspects of home will be recognized in classroom areas where things from home come into school. Recently, one nursery set up with the children an area that represented 'home'. Soon this was full of toys, books, cushions, all sorts of artefacts and the pictures that they took using their disposable cameras. They photographed their bedrooms, brothers and sisters, pets, grandparents, all the things that represented 'home' to them. The area was never without children in it – they happily explored their own and other children's home lives. The parents and carers took the lead in this; it was with their help that the teachers and the teaching assistants learned about the children's life beyond school. This rich experience gave the teacher the knowledge to inform the teaching that school staff undertook to teach the skills that children needed in the new world of Nursery. They worked in a more equal partnership with parents and carers, finding ways to bridge home and school learning for each child (Cook, 2005). The recognition that the journey for each child will be different is a feature of the guidance approach. In contrast the need for conformity will mean that the controlling approach will centre on formal sets of rules and procedures.

Teach less, more thoroughly

Coverage of the curriculum is important, but trying to cover everything means that much of what is taught is without depth. However, this is not to deny the importance of completeness in any subject. Rather, it suggests that an in-depth understanding of subject concepts and factual knowledge is more important than superficial coverage of the whole discipline.

In a guidance approach one aspect of the teacher's role is to spend time making possible the learning of 'the hard to grasp bit'. In every subject there are some concepts, some processes and some skills that can be hard to grasp. The guidance approach recognizes that some children are resistant to challenge. This means that for them it is important to avoid indicating that what they are doing is hard to learn. You will want to be encouraging, the feedback phrase 'You are working hard' will often be heard whilst they are learning. You will want to celebrate success by telling them 'You're clever at this now.' Other children relish challenge and it increases their confidence when they are set problems to solve. The guidance approach requires that teachers are inventive in the way they meet the individual's needs in a class setting.

Teach children how to learn

The internal dialogue that goes on when anyone learns anything is really important. This is prioritized in guidance approaches. Children need to know that talking about what they are learning is part of the learning process. They need to know that 'talking in the head' is part of the learning process. Working in pairs and small groups to solve particular problems is a powerful way of modelling this. When you use a guidance approach you will share with pupils the knowledge they have about how subjects work; together teacher and learners will explore with them all the things that make each distinctive, for example, the language of the topic, its concepts, theory, philosophy, processes and procedures. At the same time you will be developing with the children ways of talking about what they know, how they do tasks and how they know whether they have done well or badly, and what their successes and failures mean for the next step in learning.

Checking what each child knows about the topic is quite a challenge. Your subject knowledge has to be sound. Making some assumptions about what children should know is one way to do this. The child's learning record is often a useful starting place. In this story the teacher knows that most of the children have a fair phonic knowledge; she is concerned to find out how they can apply this to reading words. She set the task up to review which children could blend letters:

> In a class of seven-year-olds children are having a fun time
> learning to blend letter sounds. To start the task the teacher
> has some letter cards large enough for everyone to see with
> 'p', 't' and 'a'. The children in turn are asked to name the
> letter and its sound. Their initial responses to this task are
> noted by the teaching assistant. The next step is for three
> children to come to the front with the letters in the right
> order for the word 'tap'. Between them, the children sort this
> out. At this stage they are in a line but about three paces
> between each child with the letters in the right order. The
> letters 't' and 'a' are moved closer together with all the
> children saying the sound for 't' and 'a' until 'ta' are linked –
> the children saying 'ta' and the letter children linking arms.
> Next 'p' in moved to make 'tap'. Then they tried 'pat', 'apt';
> then 'n' substituted for 'p'. [N.B. You'll see that this gives one
> non-word 'nat' which is a useful indicator about the children's
> understanding of what is and is not a word.]

During the task the teaching assistant observed and recorded which children could blend three-letter words and which could not. Later, the assistant and the teacher used individual reading records to confirm what they had observed. They now had some sound data about which children would need to learn this aspect of reading. So far this could be either a control or a guidance approach. In the guidance approach, the next step was to work with each child to confirm their knowledge about this skill. The control approach would probably jump to a teaching programme for all the children who could not blend.

Summary

This chapter is about the implications that arise from two of the approaches that adults use when working with children. We have put a strong case for the use of a guidance approach by contrasting locus of control, teacher's goals and views about children and their learning, and the adult's status. Even when the teacher's preference is for this approach, we recognize that the control approach will be used frequently. Many experienced teachers who sincerely hold guidance views will often use control approaches. It is a real dilemma that we can hold and act on the two approaches almost simultaneously. This is why we asked you to work out your preferred approach. Being convinced about the value of one approach will not stop you from using the other approach. Rather it means that you will use the more appropriate approach by choice, not happenstance, knowing that the way you act has an effect on children's learning. We would predict that your choice would be the guidance approach with its emphasis on support for each child's learning. We would expect you to learn to use open formative assessment, to teach each subject thoughtfully choosing those areas which need thoroughly to be mastered and supporting children as they talk about the learning process and the choices they need to make to satisfy their internal needs.

6 The daily formative process: assessment at the centre of learning

Introduction

Formative assessment is important because it completes the teaching cycle. You plan to achieve a piece of learning. You teach what you want the pupils to achieve and how they will be able to do this. The pupils engage in tasks to support the learning objective. This is not the end. Through the teaching and the tasks there is an interchange between you and the pupils which facilitates their learning. This is a formative assessment activity in itself. You collect information from the lesson and from their work as to how far they have met the objective. At this point you make another assessment or evaluation of the success of the learning. To continue the cycle you need to act upon this assessment or evaluation in planning your next interaction with your pupils. The formative assessment, immediate or reflective, is a crucial part of an effective teaching process because it allows the teacher to match teaching and responses to the needs and understanding of individuals. This, in turn, will enable the individual to understand and secure the learning.

It will be more effective if pupils are given time to respond to feedback. The guidance approach assumes that pupils need to become engaged in what the feedback is telling them and to take individual action to enhance their own understanding and performance. By strengthening pupils' abilities to think things through for themselves and really engage in discussions, they become more engaged in their own learning. Teaching them to self-assess gives them strategies to progress their own learning. All this has implications for how teachers organize the curriculum and how he or she operates in lessons. There are implications for planning to:

- create time to respond to feedback;

- create situations where there is greater participation and thinking by pupils;

- create pupils who are involved in their own learning.

To achieve more effective learning we need to look closely at the strategies which support this taking place in the classroom.

The first thing is to believe that what children are learning and how they are learning should be used to help them learn more. This will mean that you will want to create a situation where there are opportunities for you to act upon your findings. This will not be easy when there is pressure to move on. Time needs to be allocated in which there is an opportunity to respond to individual needs. This can be done in several ways. The following are some of the ideas emerging from the assessment for learning lobby (Black and Wiliam, 1998; Torrance and Pryor, 1998; Clarke, 2003; Hall and Burke, 2003).

Imagine each child sitting in class working from their own textbook all day long. The book becomes the teacher. Think how sterile these experiences would be. There is a role for individual study programmes and it is an important part of independent learning but it is not sufficient. We have come to recognize that most children construct their knowledge through interaction with others in social contexts. We need to construct an assessment model that taps into this knowledge. To enhance their own understanding and performance children need both

Develop children's ability to think for themselves

Children become more engaged in discussion
about what and how they learn

Children become more engaged in their own learning

Figure 6.1 Increasing children's autonomy in learning

to engage in what the feedback is telling them and to take appropriate action. The idea is to create a virtuous cycle in which children become increasingly more able to know what they know, what they need to know and how they learn. (See Figure 6.1.)

By strengthening children's abilities to think things through for themselves and really engage in discussions, they become more engaged in their own learning. Teaching them to self-assess gives them strategies to progress their own learning. All this has implications for how the curriculum is organized and how teaching sessions operate. To achieve more effective learning we need to look more closely at the strategies which support this taking place in the classroom. You will want to create situations where there are opportunities for you to do this. Classrooms are busy places, there is always a great deal to do and too little time to do it. If the formative assessment cycle is going to be central to learning this means that we have to consider how we use time in the classroom, how we respond to children's learning, how we encourage autonomy and how we encourage participation.

The day-to-day promotion of formative assessment as a process

The assessment for learning lobby (Black and Wiliam, 1998) suggests formative assessment should be seen as an essential part of an effective teaching cycle. The planning and teaching phases are clearly needed to operate in the classroom but the assessment phase is often viewed as occasional and summative in nature. This is possibly because it feels like effective teaching because you are busy and the children are busy and it appears productive. Also, formative assessment has become too closely tied to an image of informal summative activities and the belief that an adequate assessment response is being made already. It is therefore important to consider more closely the contribution of formative assessment to the teaching cycle.

If assessment is viewed as a process it involves the collection of data, the analysis of those data and the use of the data to inform a particular audience. At this point it could be labelled as summative.

collect data – analyse data – report data

In Chapter 1 we have described what happens when this is for official purposes. National test results can be reported and become public property subject to scrutiny and comment. When pupils do tests in class, the results are passed back to them, for example, when a pupil gains 8/10 for a comprehension test. In both these cases, the data are collected and analysed as summative assessment. Both may have formative connotations if the pupils are expected to respond to the results and improve their performance. In the process of formative assessment there must be an indication of how the pupils can improve on their performance. For this to happen, the data must not just be analysed but also evaluated and, most important, a decision made about action to be taken.

collect data – analyse data – evaluate data – propose action

The next step is to take action. How often is an action suggested and time in the curriculum provided to follow up that action? At this point the child should be considering: 'I can do better by. . .' This is an indication to the child that they can improve on their performance. To be used formatively, the data must be analysed, evaluated and a decision made about what action to take. With the high expectations to deliver a large amount of content in the National Curriculum (DfES, 2000), teachers are often pressured to move on to the next topic. It is rather like the Mad Hatter's Tea Party where Alice barely manages a mouthful of food before she is urged to 'Move on, move on', by the Mad Hatter.

Looking again at a model for formative assessment, a further step should be added – time to respond. (See Figure 6.2.) In some ways, response time is not the last step because the teacher will immediately begin to collect data again to see if the pupil/pupils have understood so it becomes a cycle of formative assessment.

This cycle operates on various levels, at various speeds and with different groups, which is probably why it is so difficult to capture. On one level it could be an evaluation and response to the medium-term planning. An example of this can be found in the proposed assessment days at the end of each half-term in the National Numeracy Strategy (DfES, 1999). Here are two days

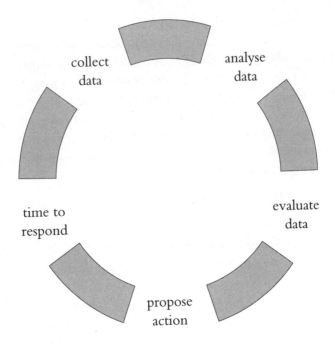

collect
data

analyse
data

time to
respond

evaluate
data

propose
action

Figure 6.2 The formative assessment cycle

in which data can be collected to inform the next half-term's planning.

At another level it could be about the whole-class response to a particular lesson. Maybe they understood something really quickly and you decide to accelerate through the next two lessons in one. Or maybe it is the other way round and the class are finding a topic difficult so you decide to make the next lesson a review rather than moving on.

At yet another level it could be that several children have had a particular problem with their homework so time is put aside to discuss this problem. This might be paralleled with any marking of work. Is time put aside to address the errors, misconceptions and comments which arise from marking a piece of work, and how is that time structured? It can be a very sterile experience being asked to correct something you know you cannot do! Corrections often need some supportive teaching in order to make the activity worthwhile.

What about the response time required for individual pupils' targets or action plans? Another formative situation which needs to be considered is when the teacher is working in the class. Every interaction with a pupil provides information which the teacher acts upon. This is formative assessment in its most short-term and immediate form. How do we as teachers best deal with these situations?

Summary

For formative assessment to be successful it is about creating a classroom in which children become engaged in learning which is meaningful to them and that you and they have strategies to respond to their learning needs.

For this to happen action needs to be taken at various levels from initial planning, adjusting daily planning through to responding to pupil needs from minute to minute through the lesson. To create a classroom where formative assessment has maximum opportunity to occur may require some fundamental rethinking of the way you organize your teaching.

The next chapters look more closely at actions which can be taken to enable effective formative assessment to take place.

7 Creating time to assess formatively

Introduction

One of the key issues in ensuring formative assessment is effective is creating time for pupils to respond to feedback. This can be done in various ways:

- Adjusting medium-term planning as a result of evaluating progress.

- Adjusting lesson plans as a result of evaluating the lesson.

- Allowing response time for homework and other marking.

- Allowing response time for individual targets.

- Responding to individuals in class.

Having identified these as actions which will allow formative assessment to operate and individual learning to take place, the next stage is to look in detail at how it is possible to operate in a way that allows this to happen. How can you find time to respond to each of thirty pupils? It helps if every interaction with a pupil is thought of as an opportunity for formative assessment. Also formative assessment is not always a one-to-one activity. And assessment can take place between pupils and as a self-assessment process. This chapter considers how you can create time in your planning and teaching to allow formative assessment responses to happen.

Adjusting medium–term planning

There is considerable pressure in many schools to complete the curriculum prescribed for the year. The formal examination system drives schools and teachers to try and ensure that all the pupils have experienced topics which may appear in test papers. Viewing this positively, having a National Curriculum means that pupils will have similar opportunities; the variations, repetitions and the slowness of delivery that occurred sometimes in the past have now gone. Set against this is the worry that the pace of delivery may not be right for all the pupils in the class. For some subjects and topics, the single pace might be appropriate because pupils can respond at their own level and have a learning experience. For other topics, a single pace is clearly not appropriate. Either the pace is too slow because some pupils learn very quickly, or the pace is too fast and some pupils never quite consolidate the learning sufficiently to recall or apply the knowledge. In your medium-term plans you need to identify the areas where differentiation needs to be provided.

The National Numeracy Strategy (DfES, 1999) has two days each half-term for review and these are vital, because they allow time for the teacher to work with the pupils (see Table 7.1). This is the time to question achievement: 'Have they grasped certain objectives?' The response to these data is to plan the level of entry into topics in the next half-term. This is possible within the National Numeracy Strategy because the curriculum is 'spiral' in design and topics are revisited at an increasingly developed level, sometimes as often as six times in a year.

These half-term review points can be usefully supplemented by putting comments on the weekly planner or medium-term plan to indicate where you would like to pick up this work with the groups next time you visit this topic.

Table 7.1 An extract from NNS long-term plans
(see www.standards.dfes.gov.uk/numeracy/publications/planning/)

Unit	Days	Pages	Topic
1	3	8–19	Place value, ordering, estimating, rounding
		76–7	Reading numbers from scales
2–3	10	24–9	Understanding + and –
		32–41	Mental calculation strategies (+ –)
		66–9	Money and 'real-life' problems
		58–61	Making decisions, checking results
4–6	13	70–7	Measures, including problems
		80–9	Shape and space
		62–5	Reasoning about shapes
7	2		Assess and review
8	5	2–7	Counting, properties of numbers
		62–5	Reasoning about numbers
9–10	10	46–51	Understanding × and ÷
		54–7	Mental calculation strategies (× ÷)
		66–9	Money and 'real-life' problems
		58–61	Making decisions, checking results
11	5	20–3	Fractions
12	5	24–9	Understanding + and –
		32–41	Mental calculation strategies (+ –)
		71, 79	Time, including problems
		58–61	Making decisions, checking results
13	5	90–3	Handling data
14	2		Assess and review
Total	60		

Telling the time:

    Group A: Ready for word problems and practical application.

    Group B and Group C: Briefly review hours and minutes.

    Group D: Re-introduce hours and minutes and read clock over next few weeks.

As you can see, topics are being covered but at an appropriate level of understanding for each group. It also picks up on individuals who seem to have a barrier to learning. The written note is there as a reminder to act. It is sometimes wiser, if pupils are stuck, to move on and return later to a topic. There is little point in 'flogging a dead horse'. Sometimes it is necessary to go back a few steps because either the child has missed a piece of knowledge or has a misconception, sometimes both. These actions are decisions teachers need to make in the light of the evidence before them. Moving on to something new can revive interest. If you monitor what has been covered and what needs to be revisited you will cover the curriculum.

Using formative assessment in the lesson and lesson evaluation

If we begin by considering the planning of a lesson there will already be factors taken into account to ensure that you provide a meaningful learning situation for the pupils in the class. Your medium-term plans will give continuity and progression. These are based on the requirements of agreed curricula and school policies. For the lesson the ability of the pupils will influence the pace and level of the work. You will have considered other factors such as the number of pupils, their self-discipline and attitude, the time, time of day and available resources, including how you will use other adults, teaching assistants and volunteers. All these will affect how you choose to organize the lesson.

Having planned the lesson, you then set out to teach it. The main purpose of this stage is that the pupils learn. During the lesson you will provide information and tasks to enable learning to take place. Sometimes the pupils are expected to engage in these tasks by themselves, sometimes in groups with peer support and sometimes with the support of an adult. Nearly all the time the teacher, teaching assistants and other adults will be engaged in supporting that learning. You will be monitoring, alert to these questions:

What are they learning?
How are they learning?

Answers to these questions will be a form of data collection. You will be receiving information from your co-workers and, of course, from the pupils. As you mark, listen and respond, you are engaging in rapid formative assessment. You are tailoring your answers and developing further questions to individuals, to a group or to the whole class.

A third stage of the process is the evaluation stage. After the lesson is finished you will consider how effective the lesson was in enabling the pupils to learn. You will consider your own input as well as the pupils' achievements. There may be marking to do, written feedback to give, informal notes to make and possibly some formal recording of their achievements. As a result of your evaluation you will come up with actions, targets for yourself and your pupils. These need to be fed back into the next set of planning.

Evaluation

The lesson was to identify the main characters in a story. The tasks involved group work to list main characters, other characters and begin to decide how the main characters influence the story. This was predominantly an oral lesson, the recording was limited to lists of the characters (pupils' task) and in the plenary the beginning of an action plan to decide how each character makes the story work. The evaluation noted what had

Table 7.2 Evaluation

Lesson	Objective	Date
English	To identify the main characters	20/4/05

Effectiveness of the lesson to meet the objective

Next time for the first lesson I would create smaller groups as some pupils did not contribute to the discussion. The groups with adults were better, as individuals were targeted, but there was little peer–peer discussion.

Pupils' learning

Task appropriate for Groups 1 and 4, who understood the task with minimum of help. Group 3 needed Teaching Assistant's support.

Individual lists which accurately recorded main characters from everyone except AD, RH and BW.

Plenary showed that Groups 2 and 3 were unsure about the actions of the main character. Group 4 had clearly grasped the concept but muddled the detail. Group 5 pupils understood and need to progress.

My teaching strategies

Next lesson:

Less introductory talk from me.

To consider less scaffolding with Group 3 – talk to TA about how. Possibly use prompt questions to support thinking.

Review actions by doing a similar activity in pairs (lesson 3?).

been achieved and how the lesson went. The data were drawn from the teacher's direct observations, the feedback from co-workers and from the pupils, and from marking the written work. Table 7.2 shows the brief evaluation.

This information is the starting place for the planning of the next lesson. The next phase of planning is more complicated than the first because you now need to reconcile the needs of progressing the medium-term planning with the needs that have arisen from the evaluation of the previous lesson. The next lesson might need to include some target setting for groups, revisiting areas of difficulty, addressing shared misconceptions, dealing with individual problems and setting adjusted objectives in the light of pupil performance. This might include deciding to move on more quickly with one group or deciding to go over old ground with another group because they have forgotten or are confused.

Because needs begin to diversify at this stage, planning becomes difficult and inevitably becomes a compromise between individual and whole-class requirements. Otherwise, taken to its ultimate conclusion, each pupil would be on an individual programme. This would be impossible to manage in a class situation and may not be beneficial anyway. It is possible to run some individual targets alongside whole-class objectives. Thought needs to be put into what are suitable targets and when they can be addressed. Careful management of your teaching assistant and other adults in the class can be part of the solution.

Allowing response time for homework remarks and other marking

If you have marked pupils' work then some time must be used to discuss the feedback. Not to do so is to miss an important teaching opportunity. As you mark, note names of pupils who have made the same error or have the same misconception. You will probably choose to address this with the whole class. You will want to start by giving credit for the work that demonstrated

Table 7.3 Next lesson with reference to evaluation

Time	Introduction	Resources
10 mins (total)	Review main characters (5 mins)	Group 5's list Book White board
	A. Review actions of main characters: 3 examples	
	B. Set Group 5 task – careful reading to fill in the chart of what happens, when and who is involved	Tablet for Group 5 Parent helper
	C. Do one example with Groups 1, 2, 3 and 4	Tablets for each group
20 mins	Group work Group 3 AD, RH, BW review main characters then today's task	5 Supervised by parent 3 supervised by TA Teacher AD, RH, BW then other groups

learning and for the effort that pupils have put in before discussing errors.

In the lesson on main characters the teacher uses accurate work from one group of pupils to review learning and provide examples for pupils who need more input. There are various ways of sorting out errors and misconceptions. One way is to draw upon those who understood to help clarify the issue. You may choose to get pupils to work in pairs to help each other. In this case the teacher reminds the pupils about how well they all know the story and works briefly with all groups, except Group

5. You may ask the teaching assistant to work with particular pupils. In this lesson the weakest group, Group 3, gets the teaching assistant, she will give less help than in session 1 but be there to monitor process and product. The group mostly likely to succeed is Group 5. Today the teacher asks a parent helper to supervise this group. (Group 5 have a task that is at the same level but uses an unfamiliar story, this gives them some challenge but does not allow the gap between these children and the rest to widen too much.) Or you may ask the teaching assistant to supervise other work while you try to unravel the barrier to learning in Group 3. In the lesson what the teacher did was to work with three individuals and then with the Groups 1, 2 and 4, supervising, supporting, asking questions, monitoring and gathering data.

You may choose to get pupils to work in pairs to help each other. This is to be this teacher's approach in the third lesson. You may ask for a corrected response such as, do two more calculations or, write another sentence. In this way, the pupils really have to come to grips with the idea and produce a successful response, possibly with the help of their peers. Pupils who have understood what they are learning are set problem-solving tasks that use their new knowledge. Pupils who are still learning are given support and time to gain the knowledge, concepts and skills. This is differentiation in action: as far as possible everyone in the class moves on to new learning at the same time.

Feedback should be, wherever possible, a celebration of success. If you ask a pupil to share their good work, this boosts the confidence of those chosen and they provide a good model to those who may not have achieved the same standard. Building on this you might choose to have another visit to the work or set a closely aligned task where the ideas can be transferred. Pupils appreciate the work of their peers and often listen very closely, as long as they can hear properly. Pupils in Group 5 made a correct list of main characters, they identified the pages in the story where these characters did something or reacted. The teacher uses their model. This gives them public credit and provides an excellent model for the other pupils. Models of good work are very helpful when pupils are stuck. They also provide class contribution to the learning, particularly in the example given, where the work is used as a stimulus for further work. Here, there is a sense of real contribution to the learning.

For the lesson about identifying the main characters and their actions, the teacher might have considered the organization in the following way:

> Before the lesson there is a five-minute briefing for the adults who take part. They are given responsibilities and asked to note particular responses for which pupils should be given credit. Here is the teacher's use of time for the main part of lesson 2:

> 13 minutes introduction, task setting;
> 2 minutes monitoring of groups and settling pupils to task;
> 8 minutes with three pupils who needed some additional input;
> 6 minutes survey of each group's activity level, feedback for on-task behaviour;
> 4 minutes sitting with Group 2, questioning, listening, getting pupils to clarify ideas;
> 7 minutes plenary with each group reporting on one thing they found out and setting homework task.

Again, the data for the next lesson have been collected and an initial evaluation made about what will happen in the next session. After the lesson, co-workers, the teaching assistant and the parent make their contribution to the lesson evaluation. The homework that was set added some more information. All the data feed into planning the next session.

Allowing response time for individual targets

So far, the time created has been for responses to work set or the ongoing learning objective. In many schools students are given targets to achieve. Often these targets are things they have been struggling with; the teacher feels that they should spend more time on them. Whilst this indicates to the pupil what they need to achieve, often the opportunity to work on the targets is left to spare moments in lessons or there is an expectation they will receive support at home. Such a target might be to practise some spellings.

Realistically, these targets will be challenging as they are something the pupil already has difficulty with and therefore has failed to learn first time round. Setting the target is not enough. The pupil will need to know how to go about realizing the target. Discussing strategies for achievement would help. Time should be given to allow children to work on their targets. This may involve independent work. Another strategy may be paired work with another pupil who understands how to provide support. All these actions imply the need for regular slots in the timetable.

Current practices vary from annual target setting, termly target setting to the setting of more immediate or ongoing targets (see Chapter 3). Setting the targets is the easy part; developing strategies for achievement, allowing time for working on them and checking that they have been achieved is the other 75 per cent of the process and time. Only if the process is followed through is it likely to work. Pupils are quick to work out where they have to respond and what they can leave to slide off the agenda. Their individual needs may not always match with the curriculum and what you would like them to achieve. Or they may be motivated by performance rather than learning goals (see the Appendix). All these are factors in thinking through the complexities of managing the learning through target setting.

Responding to individuals in class

Feedback is not only something offered as the result of finished work. All the time the teacher and other adults observe and question pupils, their responses can be classified as a form of feedback. It is quick, it is spontaneous, it is unrecorded, but it is feedback and therefore a form of formative assessment. Questions and answers are an example of instant feedback. The style of questioning will influence the type and length of answer and this is an area which can be developed so that pupils engage more in thinking and discussing (see Chapter 9). Time must be given to allow this to happen. If you only schedule enough time to give information, any questions you ask will probably be perfunctory and closed.

Summary

To allow for the complete cycle of assessment to feed into learning you need to consider how you can create time for pupils to respond to your feedback. This creation of time occurs at the planning stage as well as during the teaching. Good use of other adults in the classroom can allow well-targeted responses to individuals. Having created the time slots, they need to be used to respond to pupils' needs. These can only be discerned and planned for if you are collecting and evaluating data about their learning.

8 Creating opportunities for greater participation

Introduction

Engaging pupils in learning is fundamental to their success. If you believe that engagement comes from developing a process which includes interaction, contribution from the teacher and the pupils, feedback and goal setting, then formative assessment is part of this process. To get the best from an interactive model of involvement you will need to address issues of teaching style, the nature of the tasks set, the response to those tasks and the way in which you expect the pupils to work. This chapter explores these issues as part of a classroom set-up where formative assessment can function with success.

Teaching strategies to encourage discourse

Consider the control approach where the teacher provides an explanation of how to reach the objective and then sets work from a textbook or worksheet. Apart from marking, it is difficult to find opportunities to collect information about the pupils' understanding. Greater discourse between teacher and pupil, and pupil and pupil, increases the chances of collecting better data on which to base formative assessment. Importantly it also

Table 8.1 A didactic introduction

Learning objective: to be able to name and match OS map symbols to grid references

Time	Introduction	Resources
10 mins	• Establish learning objective • Demonstrate on board how to establish 4- and 6-figure grid reference (review) • Find 6-figure reference on board, identify symbol • Refer to key to establish meaning of symbol • Instruct how to do task	Grid drawn on board with 3 map symbols
	Development Whole class, working individually with map and symbol sheet (share key) Record in books	30 worksheets of map and 10 symbols. 15 photocopies of OS key

provides immediate opportunities to clarify understanding by using the guidance approach to promote learning. This suggests that it is a high priority to create as many opportunities as possible for discussion. This is likely to enhance the process of learning in two ways: by creating a shared understanding and by providing the teacher with data about the pupils' understanding on which the teacher can act more effectively. Where guidance approaches are central, discourse (sometimes called learning conversations or talk about learning) is important because it develops three interlinked areas: your teaching strategies, the activities you give and the strategies for learning you expect pupils to use.

Table 8.2 An interactive introduction

Learning objective: to be able to name and match OS map symbols to grid references

Time	Introduction	Resources
20 mins	• Establish learning objective • Review 6-figure references by asking children to demonstrate Ask children the steps taken: First 2 figs Horizontal first Final figs tenths of the square • How do we know what the symbol means? Where do we look? • Using key sheet, in pairs find these symbols • Instruct class on task	Grid drawn on board with 3 map symbols 15 photocopies of OS key sheet
	Development	
	• Working in mixed-ability pairs: On blank grid, draw a symbol, draw again below with name and 6-fig grid reference	20 cards with a symbol on each 20 blank grids with space below

If pupils are given opportunities to talk about learning and how learning takes place they will begin to be able to think about how they learn. It is thought that successful learners 'talk in their head', which is a form of metacognition. Tasks that involve listening and talking about the work begin to allow this learning to go on. In the first extract (see Table 8.1) the teaching input is purely instructional. The teacher explains how the pupils can succeed but the way the teacher presents the teaching input is strongly didactic. There is no opportunity for interaction. A model is offered which pupils are then required to repeat in individual work. This is likely to lead to the teacher using a control approach.

In the next extract the same teaching input is approached in a different way (see Table 8.2). This time notice how the teacher has used the pupils to demonstrate. Notice how the teacher intends to involve the pupils through questioning and a paired task. The more practical participation will keep the pupils' interest. At the same time it allows them to model part of what they are going to be asked to do. This will let them get started on the task when it is set. Note how questioning of 'how?' generates the steps they need to think about and take. This lesson will tend to allow the teacher to use a guidance approach.

At this point it is worth mentioning that the task that the teacher has set is likely to be right for the children. Tasks that are likely to be successful have these characteristics: they are real for the individuals, within the experience of the children, presented clearly and concrete (Nuttall, 1987). This last point, Nuttall (1987) argues, means that you will set tasks that let the child see what he or she has learned and what might need to be learned next. The task you set will allow you to feedback and work with children in order for them to develop strategies for learning. When they are making, doing and talking, each task will form part of the information you need to help them to understand their own learning and choose strategies that are likely to be successful.

Clear learning objectives

Part of a successful lesson is to have clear learning objectives. The pupils need to know what they are expected to learn by the end of the lesson. If the objectives are clear to the pupils they will know what they are aiming for and when they have been successful. This might be done by writing the objective on the board or by telling the children what you expect them to achieve. Clarke (2001) lays great emphasis on clearly stated objectives. If you are to ask children to reflect on their own learning then they have to know what they are expected to learn. By posting clear goals pupils will be able to say whether they understand by the end of the lesson or by the end of a series of lessons. This Year 2/3 teacher explains what happens when the learning objective is not clear:

> There is no point you doing this with a child and the child doesn't know, who's sitting there sort of looking up in the air, probably doesn't understand what you're giving them, what you're delivering to them. Children have got to know. . . and understand what they're doing. . . because how can you go forward if the child hasn't understood what they've had before. Therefore the teacher assessment is there to see whether the children actually do know what they're meant to be doing. . . You've got to know that the child is understanding and able to do so. Your assessment is by seeing so that the child can progress. (Torrance and Pryor, 1998, p.33)

But a clear objective will not be sufficient. It will be necessary to indicate *how* the objective can be achieved. This helps the pupil to find a way forward and can be likened to the 'strategy' or 'how' part of target setting. The two lesson extracts above address the 'how' with different teaching styles but in both extracts the process of going about the learning is clearly explained. By the end of the lesson the pupils should be able to read and create a 6-figure grid reference and know how to name the OS map symbols. These are two pieces of knowledge which they will be able to use again in map-reading contexts. The 'how you do it' is vital for their success. It is essential to have strategies for the process of learning. You need to give them strategies for the learning.

Both Headington (2003) and Clarke (2001) ask 'how will children know when they have achieved what the teacher asks for?' Clarke refers to 'success criteria' which are about conveying to the children the way they will know that they have successfully responded to the learning situation. She also warns that success criteria need to be clearly separated from the instructions about completing tasks: 'Teachers need to separate the task instructions clearly from the learning intention and success criteria, or children can begin their work without knowing clearly the difference between what you want them to do and what you want them to learn' (Clarke, 2001, p.21). The success criteria for the map tasks will be to do with accuracy in identifying symbols by grid references, the last bullet point in the instruction.

To gain clarity for the teaching input section you could consider that there are three elements to its structure: sharing the learning objective, the teaching input on how children will achieve the learning and finally instructions for supporting tasks. The pupils' success criteria will be closely aligned with your assessment criteria (see Table 8.3).

This is not the only model you might choose to use. But as pupils need a mixture of objectives, it is an appropriate model, because it lets you concentrate with them on skill building. Bear in

Table 8.3 The structure of an introduction and teaching input

Learning objective:		
Time	**Introduction**	**Resources**
20 mins	• Sharing of learning objective	
	• How/teaching input	
	• Instruction for task	
	• Task	

Table 8.4 Modelling a stage of problem-solving

Learning objective: to have a strategy for getting started on a scientific problem

Time	Introduction	Resources
30 mins	• Working out how to solve the problem of what the essential ingredients of cakes are (flour, sugar, eggs, margarine, water)	Ingredients sufficient for 10 small cakes
	• As the discussion progresses list key decisions on board	
	• What goes into cakes? Where will we find that information? (making sense of the question)	
	• These are the ingredients (list/actual ingredients)	Ingredients list
	• Prediction: what do you think they do? E.g. if we left out the milk what would the cake be like? (prediction)	Flip chart and Blu-Tack
	• What else might make a difference? (balance of ingredients) How can we find out? (cakes with different quantities of ingredients) Setting up an experiment (choosing a way forward) (keep time as non-variable)	
	• Being systematic	
	• Recap list of useful actions	
	• Share out the different recipes to groups to set up	Recipe sheets with missing quantities
	Group tasks of cake mixing	Equipment, ingredients

Table 8.5 Applying problem-solving skills

Learning objective: to have a strategy for getting started on a scientific problem

Time	Introduction	Resources
	• Working out how to solve the problem of what the essential ingredients of cakes are (flour, sugar, eggs, margarine, water)	Victoria sponge recipe
	• I am having a problem with my cake-making: they either turn out runny or like crunchy biscuits. What is going wrong?	
	• Guided discussion on variables (time, cake-tin size, balance of ingredients, cooking time, place in the oven)	
	• In groups of 5, each group designs an experiment to deal with one of these variables	
	Group tasks of cake mixing	Equipment required Ingredients required

mind that too many prescribed 'hows' do not lead to development of decision-making and independence. To encourage children's selection of how to do things, you could choose to support their decision-making. Over time you will reduce the amount of support until they need little or no input from you. This is the use of scaffolding in the guidance approach. Even with young children it is very successful approach. Its strength lies in discussing how you make the decisions: 'I think I'll do it this way

Table 8.6 Scaffolding the learning

Some children are set a colour-mixing task; they are all just settling into Reception, and working with a classroom teaching assistant (TA). To get them ready for the task the TA first gathers them together.

TA: We've only got three colours of paint out today. We're going to use them to make some other colours. What will we need to do first?

Chris: Um . . .

Ali: Aprons.

TA: Good, Ali, we'll need to keep clean so aprons it is. Gus, where are the aprons? Can you point to them?

Gus: Over there.

TA: Would you fetch 3 aprons, thanks, Gus?

TA Let's find out what happens if we mix blue and yellow. How will we do that?

Gus: I don't know.

Ali: Use our fingers?

TA: We could use a brush?

All three children think this over and reach for brushes.

TA: Shall we put blue in the mixing tray first?

Each child leaps into action and blue paint eventually arrives in the mixing tray.

TA: What will happen when you add yellow?

Children look blank.

TA: Will the colour still be blue?

Chris: It's green. Look, green . . .

Gus: Mine's not.

Ali: More yellow paint.

TA: You've made green. So mixing blue and yellow makes . . . ?

All three: GREEN.

---

because. . .'; modelling the decision-making process: 'First I did this, then I did . . ., next . . . and so on'; and sharing children's strategies with each other: 'Tom, can you tell Pat how you made . . .'. An early lesson in a decision-making situation might have a teaching input like that shown in Table 8.4.

In other situations where pupils have good experience of problem-solving the input might look like the one in Table 8.5. Here the children are being asked to make their own decisions about how they will go about the task. Some of this planning will be to do with the age and ability of the pupils, but a big factor will be their past experience of problem-solving and decision-making.

In an early years setting, the problem-solving will probably arise spontaneously from a pupil's activity. Table 8.6 is an example of how an adult might facilitate the thinking of the child through observational comments and questioning.

In each of the lesson extracts above, the learning objective is stated at the start of the lesson and may be displayed on the board too. You might deliberately choose to change this by setting up a stimulus or a problem and then refer to the objective after-wards. For example, reading a short story and then telling the pupils on what to focus. Exciting starts to lessons are really important. This is when pupils are motivated and become engaged . . . or not.

It might seem as if we have strayed from formative assessment but this is not so. By setting up situations where pupils have opportunities to participate, you are creating a situation where communication is two-way and immediately there is an opportunity to find out what pupils do or do not understand. As you respond to them you are making instant assessments and acting upon them.

Providing more discursive and decision-making situations through pupil working styles and task types

The way you set up the tasks and the types of task you provide can give pupils a greater role in discussion and decision-making. This, in turn, develops their skills, increases participation and allows you to observe the extent of their understanding. In the whole-class part of a lesson you might employ some of the following strategies to encourage pupil engagement:

- Mini-discussion groups with recording of ideas;

- Starting with a problem;

- Using questions to seek a viewpoint;

- Challenging a misconception;

- Questioning a homework response;

- Having a no-hands-up policy;

- Starting with a pupil question;

- Brief paired discussion before an answer is requested;

- Brief paired task with feedback expected.

The National Numeracy Strategy Vocabulary Book which can be found on www.standards.dfes.gov.uk/numeracy/publications/resources/vocabulary/ also offers some useful strategies for questioning such as:

Ask children who are getting started with a piece of work:

- How are you going to tackle this?
- What information do you have? What do you need to find out or do?

Make positive interventions to check progress while children are working, by asking:

- Can you explain what you have done so far? What else is there to do?
- Why did you decide to use this method or do it this way?
- Could there be a quicker way of doing this?

Ask children who are stuck:

- Can you describe the problem in your own words?
- Can you talk me through what you have done so far?
- Have you compared your work with anyone else's?

These are just a few of the questions offered and many can be used in the group work as well as the main teaching. The next section of the Vocabulary book considers closed and open mathematical tasks. Open tasks include:

- Tell me two numbers with a difference of 2
- What numbers can you make with 2, 3 and 6?
- What even numbers lie between 10 and 20?

One of the ways of promoting higher order thinking and involving pupils in decision-making is to open up the task (Torrance and Pryor, 1998). This might be done by changing the task to a question. Instead of you saying 'Sort these toys' you might instead say 'How can we sort these toys?' Here the expectation of engagement has been increased by asking the child to contribute to the decision-making. Such an example nicely illustrates how simple situations can be turned into better learning situations for children.

It will be possible to achieve some goals by pupils choosing their own strategy. This happens in time set for activities such as writing journals (Graham and Johnson with Bearne, 2003). In journals the children are free to play with their writing. This is a serious venture, at first arising from a concern to get boys more involved in writing. Writing journals allows children space to write where there are no demands about topic, or genre, or style or form or, indeed, correctness. Furthermore, although there are opportunities to share, these notebooks are the children's own property, and, as such, not marked by the teacher. This seems somewhat alarming, especially where formative assessment is central. But the space created where children are setting their own agenda has allowed exactly the climate that is needed to observe pupils working. And, because of the trust created by the activity, most children choose to share what they write with their teachers. Having started in one school, this approach has been widely and successfully adopted throughout Croydon and in other parts of England as well. Success has been reflected in national test results but perhaps, more importantly, it has helped many pupils to think of themselves as writers.

Summary

In this chapter issues of pupil engagement have been considered and some strategies you might employ offered to ensure greater engagement. These include:

- encouraging greater discourse;

- making learning objectives clear;

- explaining to pupils how they can succeed;

- letting pupils know what that success will look like.

Consideration has been given to the idea of facilitating learning through:

- verbal support;

- decision-making tasks;

- good question strategies (which are explored further in the next chapter).

Torrance and Pryor (1998) offer a word of warning when they point out that it is easy for learning to be seen as fragmented through the use of specific learning goals and assessment criteria. They remind us of the importance of general understanding and capability which they see as more useful and longer lasting.

> Maybe learning is not this staged move from the simple to the complex; that it is more about active engagement with what they encounter and incorporate into their developing scheme. (Torrance and Pryor, 1998, p.15)

This is a very valuable comment and one which supports and drives the idea of providing a stimulating environment. This is an approach which remains live in the early years but has been lost to some extent in current primary school approaches.

9 Questioning strategies to promote engagement

Introduction

Black *et al.* (2003) identify good questioning by the teacher and the pupils as contributing to increased engagement in thinking by pupils which in turn leads to an increase in understanding. The right kinds of questions promote classroom discussion; as a result of the increased mental and social engagement, it is possible for the teacher and the pupils to be more aware of the state of the pupils' understanding. Being aware of this understanding is the first purpose of formative assessment.

If you want to know what anyone is thinking, the quickest method is to ask them. Questioning can be seen to play a strong role in the second lesson extract (Table 8.2) where the teacher plans to draw upon the pupils' contributions. Good questioning engages pupils in learning. But what is 'good' questioning? There are many types of question and it is up to you to select the appropriate type for the situation you are in. It is useful to be aware of the types of questions and to develop your repertoire. Pupils too will benefit from learning to ask useful questions.

Pupils' responses to questioning

All teachers question their pupils. A commonly observed pattern is described by Clarke (2001, p.87):

> Pupils typically leave the answering of class questions to the few who appear to be able to respond quickly, and are unwilling to risk making mistakes in public. The teacher can keep a lesson going by questioning in this way, but ultimately knows that the understanding of only a few pupils has been revealed.

Particularly, be wary of the three-part exchange in which the teacher asks a question, the pupil answers with a word or phrase, the teacher registers approval or disapproval and immediately moves on to the next question with another pupil (Brissenden, 1988). Pupils become very adept at 'playing the game'. They quickly learn the body language and phrases of rejection and many decide they will no longer volunteer answers because to do so avoids rejection (Boylan, 2004). Table 9.1 is an extract from Boylan's research in primary and secondary schools about the dynamics of the classroom when questions are being asked.

At this point ask yourself these questions about the statements in Table 9.1:

- Which of these uses a control approach?

- Which uses a guidance approach?

- What are the possible effects on your feedback from the types of strategies adopted?

- Which have you used in the classroom?

The observations about the approaches to questions indicate that it is important to develop questioning. It is most important to avoid pointless routines so that instead a classroom environment is created where all pupils are comfortable enough to contribute, even if they may not have the right answer. One way to address this is not always to rely on volunteers to answer your questions. Sometimes choose pupils who have their hands up, but also choose pupils who you would like to answer the question. There will be times when you want the whole class to respond: when you ask everyone to count in threes in a maths lesson or repeat the refrain of a poem or in a guided read in English. Whole-class responses usually keep the pupils engaged.

Table 9.1 Questioning events in the classroom

A The teacher asks a question and then gives the class time to think about an answer before they can put their hands up.	**B** Pupils don't put their hands up and then teacher asks someone by name for the answer.
C Someone calls out the answer. The teacher listens to the first person who calls out.	**D** The teacher asks pupils to discuss the answer with someone else and then asks for hands up.
E The teacher asks pupils to discuss the answer with someone else and then asks for a pair to give an answer by name.	**F** Everyone answers the question together – for example, by writing down the answer and showing it together.
G Everyone takes a turn to answer.	**H** The teacher asks a question and pupils put their hands up straightaway.
I The pupils ask the questions.	**J** The teacher does not ask questions.

A repertoire of question types

Perrott (1982) used Bloom's taxonomy (1956), which is a classification of educational objectives, to set up suitable types of question. She expands his six types of learning to indicate how teachers can use questions to promote them. Table 9.2 is a summary of Perrott's key question words alongside Bloom's classification.

As you can see from the list, questions about knowledge are those which involve recall. These depend on prior knowledge and a good memory. Usually these questions elicit short answers, they could be considered to be 'lower-order questions' because they do not require 'new' thinking. Whilst lower-order questions seek immediate and known responses, higher-order questions require pupils to think and explain their responses. When asked a simple question such as 'What is the capital of Scotland?' the response will come from a pupil's knowledge base. Either the pupil can recall the factual information or not. This is a lower-order question and only requires straight recall with no expectation to interpret or develop the information or change it in any way from how it was first learned. In many review sections of the lesson questions tend to be of this type. The teacher will start with 'Who can remember . . .' and because this is expected to be a short, quick part of the lesson the teacher will probably be inclined to seek short, non-explanatory answers. A fast sequence of lower-order questioning will gain a response from many of the class, as long as they already know the information, because you are asking them to recall known facts. Pupils who do not know the facts will not be able to take part. The questioning moves on quickly and there is no time for a 'working out' strategy. Learning is likely to be low because responses are solely dependent on knowledge already committed to memory.

When pupils have to alter or use the knowledge they possess to answer a question, the question is categorized as a higher-order

Table 9.2 Question types

Bloom taxonomy	Perrott questions	Pupil responses
Knowledge	Who?	Define
	What?	Recall
	Where?	Recognise
	When?	Name
Comprehension	Describe	Put in your own words
	Compare	Explain
	Contrast	
Application	Apply	Employ
	Classify	Give an example
	Use	Choose
Analysis	Why?	What factors?
	Draw conclusions	
	Determine evidence	
Synthesis	Predict	Produce
	Write	Develop
	What would happen if. . . ?	
Evaluation	Judge	Assess
	Decide	Justify

(Perrott, 1982, summary of pp.38–41)

question. 'Can you explain how you solved the problem?' would be a typical higher-order mathematics question. In Bloom's remaining categories, comprehension, application, analysis, synthesis and evaluation, 'thought' and 'use of knowledge' are required before a pupil is able to respond. Perrott's key words usefully point the way to how to ask questions which elicit such responses. 'Why did Fawkes and his companions want to blow up the Houses of Parliament?' or 'What would happen if you changed the number of choices on the activity rota?'

Interestingly, 'What do these map symbols represent?' might appear as a higher-order question for pupils if they have to find the key of the map to answer. It turns into a lower-order question for pupils once they know the symbols. The same is true of the Fawkes question. This is where you need to know the state of knowledge of the pupils in your class. Then selecting a particular pupil to answer your question becomes a very purposeful strategy. As a teacher it is important to realize what kind of question you have asked and, consequently, what kind of response you expect. Does a pupil need time to think? Does the pupil need time to work out an answer? In the examples given above, expected response time is going to be different, depending on the knowledge the child holds. Good teachers are usually aware of response times needed by individual pupils.

Response time

Response time is a really important factor when judging the pace of whole-class sessions. If a teacher asks a series of individuals a sequence of higher-order questions, the pace of the session is going to slow because responses will be longer and more explanatory. Think about asking pupils one after another how they worked out a particular subtraction calculation. This might be deemed appropriate in situations where there is shared engagement. On another occasion, the rest of the pupils may become disengaged from the teaching and start to find other things to do!

Rowe (1974) researched the effects of 'wait time', that is how long a teacher is prepared to wait for an answer. She found that by increasing it from the usual 0.9 seconds, three things happened: pupils began to develop longer answers, they became more confident and the number of non-responses decreased. With a longer response time pupils began to respond to each other and more explanations were offered. Generally there was an increase in discourse and encouragingly pupil–pupil discourse developed.

Black *et al.* (2003) included wait time in their research with secondary teachers with positive results. They considered that it allowed students time to think but it also raised the expectation that everyone would be able to contribute. Teachers in the project reported that it was hard to introduce but they found it worthwhile because it paid off in the long run.

Alongside the fast closed-question approach and the more prolonged higher-order questioning lies a mixture of questioning and inclusion strategies:

- asking the whole class a higher-order question and then targeting a pupil to respond;

- asking the whole class and then choosing a volunteer with their hand up;

- naming a pupil and then asking them a question;

- asking everyone to respond together;

- targeting a group.

Add to this higher- and lower-order questioning with expected response times and you will be able to adjust the pace of your teaching.

Applying questioning strategies to stages of a lesson

Teaching a new learning objective

Whole-class teaching is probably one of the most challenging situations in which to function effectively as a teacher. In front of you is a large group of pupils with a wide range of ability, varying knowledge and different speeds of working. Because of this pupils are going to vary in their responses. The main purpose is to get all the pupils to understand to a level where they are able to respond independently. This response will probably be in the form of a learning task later in the lesson.

It is important to engage and motivate the pupils at this point. Clarke (2001, p.21) refers to this when she says 'Pupils often first need to be captured at the start of the lesson, by the context and your introduction and stimulus'. Drawing the pupils in with good questioning will keep their attention and also give you feedback about their understanding as you progress. The higher-order questions such as 'why?' and 'what do you think will happen?', 'who can explain?' and 'what factors are involved here?' demand a thoughtful response from pupils. They also indicate that you want them to be part of building the new learning. It gets away from conveying the message: This is what you need to know and I (the teacher) am the only one who can inform you. The 'just do it, don't think' approach should be avoided unless you are absolutely sure that is appropriate.

In the whole-class work you may need to present different levels of work. This is mainly done through questioning past and present work at various levels of difficulty; when teaching doubling, questions could range from 'What is double 3?' to 'What is double 37?' The teaching point for everyone is 'doubling'; challenging the able pupils in the context of big numbers keeps them engaged. Offering problem contexts can be more challenging: 'Jane had seven flowers on her rose tree but within the last week the number doubled. How many flowers are there now?'

Whole-class review of a learning objective (follow-on lesson)

There are more opportunities to question and get pupils not only to recall but also apply knowledge in this phase of a lesson because they now have experiences that they can draw upon.

Group work

In the group work the questions become targeted on individuals, probing their understanding and supporting their thinking: 'How did you work that out?' and 'Is there a relationship between the data you have collected and the question you asked at the beginning?' These are the type of questions which support Bloom's (1956) classification of application, analysis, synthesis and evaluation. You are asking pupils to construct their understanding of the situation and how it might apply to other situations. In Piagetian terms this would be described as assimilation. Skemp (1971) called it relational learning. The expectation is that, as you engage with pupils in the group work, you generate more of a dialogue and become a facilitator as well as an instructor. Comments such as 'Tell me what you have done here' and 'What do you plan to do next?' should be used. Once again this is the guidance approach in action.

The plenary

The plenary can take many forms and questioning will play a part. This questioning will be at a level where pupils have an opportunity to report back on their learning. There are many variations on this. A direct question requiring a factual answer: 'James, what did you find out when you took the temperature of the water?' or, following a lesson on the gunpowder plot, a challenge: 'Can you think of any parallels in today's world where the same types of decision have been made?' The thinking in the plenary can be 'rolled over' with questions such as: 'Can you think of further examples by Friday?' A question might open the door for the next lesson: 'Can you find a story with a moral and bring it to next Monday's lesson where we will share and discuss them?'

Getting the pupils to ask the questions

If you are aiming to get the pupils to engage in their work and become self-motivated, then questioning will become an important part of their repertoire too. Therefore you need to teach the pupils to ask questions. Through discussion of appropriate questions to ask, and who to ask, you will begin to develop pupils who are capable of independent inquiry. All the strategies we have suggested can be used by pupils as well.

The quality of the questions and question sequences

Black *et al.* (2003, p. 42) found that 'More effort has to be spent in framing questions that are worth asking'. Not surprisingly students respond better if they feel the question is worth answering. The questions that they value are ones where they are expected to discuss their own understanding of an issue, when this contributes to their own learning or that contributes genuinely to a class discussion. An example of this could be the response to a 'How did you work that out?' question or 'What do you think about this situation?' or a challenging question rather like a problem: 'Why do you rarely find trees growing above 6,000 feet?' One more unusual approach is also worth considering. In one plenary a teacher engaged one pupil in a dialogue for just short of twenty minutes. The rest of the class were fascinated. The general feeling was that everyone was engaged. It was obviously a feature of this teacher's repertoire to do this regularly. It is not for every teacher though. This moves the whole discourse away from Brissenden's (1988) three exchanges pattern and the 'guess what the teacher is thinking' model.

Developing pupils' thinking through a series of questions is a powerful strategy as long as it is a genuine discourse and not 'guess what I am thinking'. Think of this in a learning situation as a question sequence used as a scaffolding tool. The questions to some extent pursue the teacher's agenda but also respond to what the pupil is offering. The teacher is really paying attention to the answers, really listening and responding.

T: What is the symbol for a church on the ordnance survey map?
P: A black square with a cross on top.
T: How do you know?
P: Just did.
T: If you didn't know, what would you do?
P: Look on the list on the side.
T: What do we call that list?
P: Is it 'the key'?
T: Yes, well done. Are churches always squares and crosses?
P: No, you can have a circle and a cross.
T: Why do you think there are two different symbols?
P: I don't know.
T: Can you guess?
P: No.
T: Can you find out and come back at the end of the lesson to tell the class?

Summary

Questioning is a key strategy in teaching and formative assessment as it promotes pupil response and engagement. As Black *et al.* (2003, p. 39) comment: 'he [the teacher] creates opportunities for the students to exchange ideas, articulate their thoughts and to fashion answers in a supportive environment'. As the pupils respond in detail to higher-order questions their conceptual understanding is revealed and the teacher is informed of their state of knowledge.

As a teacher, develop your questioning skills:

• use closed and open questions as appropriate;

- choose lower-order or higher-order questions as appropriate;
- engage in meaningful sequences to scaffold thinking;
- use a variety of question types;
- listen and respond to pupils' answers;
- get the pupils to ask questions.

10 Constructive feedback

Introduction

Making feedback positive is clearly important. This is the theme of this chapter. Feedback comes in many forms. As the Assessment Reform Group (2002) put it, 'Teachers should be aware of the impact that comments, marks and grades can have on learners' confidence and enthusiasm and should be as constructive as possible in the feedback that they give' (www.assessment-reform-group.org.uk). Even when moving round the class teachers give out subtle messages: a smile here, a frown there, the turn of the head. These slight, almost imperceptible signs, give those we teach information about how we view them. Without opening our mouths we send out messages about work and conduct. This chapter is about how to be constructive in the feedback comments that give learners the message. This information will be about success on tasks and on the process of learning. The last section in the chapter considers how pupils can develop their own self-assessment strategies.

Constructive feedback

Feedback is one of the key elements in formative assessment. If there is no feedback, there is no formative assessment, only summative assessment. Feedback can exist in many forms. It is the comments you make to pupils about their work as you conduct the lesson, it is the follow-up questions you ask them, it is the comments you write on their books when you are marking, it is the grades you award for work, it is the way you plan your follow-up lesson and it is the smile that you give to a pupil who has put in effort and been successful.

What is the effect of your feedback on those you teach? It is important that you reflect carefully on the feedback you provide to your pupils and consider what you are commenting on and the effect it has on your pupils. First, you need to consider whether your feedback is about behaviour or work. Make this clear to the pupil. It is not always easy to unwrap the messages we send out to the class. A teacher making a loud comment about the success of one pupil's work might be a message to others about being on task. One could argue that this comment is a more positive and less nagging way of getting children back on task! The words are positive but the body language is giving different message.

> The class is making cubes. Jason has not started his work.
> Teacher: (Noticing Jason but not looking at him, talks to
> Sarah who sits opposite to Jason) Sarah, you're making good
> progress. Do you know what to do next?
> Sarah: Yes, I'm going to stick it together.
> Teacher: Then what?
> Sarah: Count the edges.
> T: Excellent, you'll be finished in no time.
> (Jason listens in and finally starts the task.)
> T: Good, Jason, you'll need to be quick now you've started.
> (Teacher does not engage in conversation but moves away.
> Jason knows he has been noticed. Later, the teacher
> comments on Jason's cube.)

Here the teacher is using a control approach with Jason and a guidance approach with Sarah. Sometimes it is important to resist the impulse to comment and punish the apparent disobedience.

Making this judgement is never going to be easy. In this case the teacher decided that as Jason had started the maths task it was more productive for him to have feedback on that.

What balance of comments do you use when addressing the whole class? Sometimes classes and some lessons can push us into making lots of comments about conduct.

> The lesson has made the pupils excited and noisy.
> T: (loudly) Jack, Sam, Table 4, will you quieten down.
> (More noise)
> T: (even louder) Everyone, be quiet.
> (Noise and movement lessens)
> T: (now pleading) Now, Shamir, sit please, now . . .

We do not want end up nagging or even worse pleading for on-task behaviour. This is where using control approaches briefly and effectively can make using the guidance approach possible.

> T: (loudly) Everyone, look at me. (3-second pause) Thank-you table 2, table 3, Sally is ready. I'm really pleased with the work you're doing. We're making really useful discoveries. Look at the model that Sally's table has made. It looks very exciting. Later we'll get them to tell us about it. Now, everyone, what we're doing means that we do need to talk and move about the class. Let's do that really quietly and think carefully about what you're doing. . . You may talk quietly and look before you move. . . . Excellent, table 4, you're really thinking about how the trucks move and doing it sensibly.

Having sorted the minor disruption by reminding pupils about the behaviour that is expected it becomes easier to move to providing feedback in the form of praise. This begins to recreate a better working atmosphere where the talk between teacher and pupils focuses on the tasks.

When giving feedback, is the comment about effort or successful learning? Chaplian (2000) suggests that learners think about success in three ways. Some put it down to luck, some to ability and some to effort. If you ask children about this you will get this sort of answer, 'I think if I do better it might be because I'm lucky' or '. . . because I've worked harder.' To counter any reliance on the luck element, effort and achievement need to be recognized.

> Stuart's work is below the standard that he would normally achieve. He has, however, worked hard, so the teacher's comment is about his effort with a suggestion about how to proceed: 'Stuart, you worked really hard at your story. I like the way you've tried to use conversation. Would it help if you used the tape recorder to try out some ideas?' At the end of the week Stuart has made real progress in the area of the story that he had struggled with. Now the teacher's comment is on his achievement: 'Stuart, I liked the way the conversation in your story moved the action along. You're really getting to be good at that.'

The more we can encourage both effort and achievement aspects of work the better. This form of feedback which separates out the effort from the achievement shows that we do not expect all learning to be straightforward. It supports the need for some learning to require much effort. Again, comments about the quality and success of the work should be present as this gives the pupils an indication of their progress in learning.

Is the feedback an endpoint or can the pupils respond to it and improve their work? Sadler (1989) noted that improvement to performance does not always follow from a teacher making valid and reliable judgements about a student's work. He thinks this is because students need to know what the expected performance should be. This is a situation where examples and modelling can be helpful. Clarke (2001) indicates it is important to share the objective and the success criteria of an activity with the pupils. (This is the 'how' referred to in Chapter 8.)

Reward – valuing learning rather than grading?

Reward is an interesting topic to consider when engaging pupils in learning. If pupils are pleased that they got their spellings right they could be meeting either a learning goal or a performance goal. Dweck (1989) describes 'learning goals' as a situation where children seek to improve their competence and 'performance goals' as situations where children want to register success with others or are seeking approval. The pupils' success will be a learning goal if it meets a target that aligns with their own need. If it is because of the reward of all those ticks then the pupil might be responding to a performance goal. Dweck points out why this is important. She suggests that, depending on their goals, children have significantly different approaches to learning. She found that competition, comparison and success criteria foster a performance–goal mentality which in turn does not encourage the development of sustained self-motivated learners. She recommends engaging in task analysis, adopting challenging standards based on personal progress and focusing on past and future success with effort and strategy the reasons for success or failure. This strongly relates to an ipsative assessment approach. We want the pupil to be pleased because learning her spelling matched her learning goals (see Appendix).

Backing this view, Torrance and Pryor (1998) in their work consider that positive reinforcement strategies can lead to children actually avoiding intellectual challenge because they want to be sure of the reward. The implication is that is if we overdo the rewards pupils may choose easier tasks so they get the smiley sticker. This is certainly something to be aware of on those occasions when we use control approaches. It is possible that the practice in many primary schools of reward systems such as marbles in the jar earning extra play time, all forms of house points and stamps may focus attention on performance rather than learning goals for some, perhaps the majority of pupils. Being cautious and thoughtful about using rewards seems to be good practice.

More evidence to support this view comes from Lepper and Hodell (1989) who found that extrinsic reward systems may have detrimental effects on intrinsic motivation, particularly when the task requires a creative response rather than a routine response. They also noted that where rewards were involved children chose more attainable and less demanding activities.

Control approaches are part of the teacher's repertoire. When getting to know a new class, reward systems begin to set the working atmosphere that marks successful classrooms. Again, using a control approach with well-thought-through reward systems can be extremely effective in beginning to manage some of the challenging behaviours that some children have. The key seems to be about managing the move from control to guidance approaches. Teachers need to be skilful in moving from a reliance on external rewards to the guidance approach which will, in the longer term, allow individual greater self-motivation and self-regulation.

Feedback during the session

Feedback is not only something offered as the result of finished work. All the time the teacher and other adults observe and question children, their responses can be classified as a form of feedback. It is quick, it is spontaneous, it is unrecorded but it is feedback and therefore a form of formative assessment. Pupils are remarkable in their ability to understand unspoken messages about their success or failure. The body language and the phrases a teacher uses when pupils have given an incorrect answer are soon learned by them; they adjust their behaviour as a response. The teacher did not address Jason's off-task behaviour, but talked to another child. The apparently throw-away remark, 'Good, Jason, you'll need to be quick now you've started', is 'read' by Jason for what it is; praise for on-task behaviour. He has understood this reaction by the teacher to his conduct. The next time he is involved in off-task behaviour as the teacher comes towards him we may expect that he will get busy on the task.

Feedback needs to be about the learning. If one of the learning objectives is to provide neat work then it is appropriate to comment on neatness. If it is not, then it should not be part of the feedback; the comment should relate to the learning objective. Try to make facilitating remarks that enable the pupil to move forward. The learning outcomes for the cube lesson were about counting edges and planes, not about sticking and neatness. The teacher's feedback concentrates on the things like accuracy in counting the edges; comment on neatness is avoided. It is useful if you can link your comments to success against the 'how' as well as learning objective. Make accurate assessments and provide feedback about:

- the learning process – how does the pupil learn?

- progress towards learning objectives – what is the pupil learning?

The pupils on table 4 have just said that the truck goes faster down a 10 per cent slope than a 5 per cent slope. At this point the teacher is not over-concerned about the accuracy of their observations but on the process they used.

Teacher: How did you work that out?
J: We used the stop watch.
Teacher: Is that all you did? Take me through what you did.
SL: Slope and bricks.
Tom: We measured the slope with (waves a protractor). . .
J: That was tricky, using the protractor took ages.
Teacher: Why was that?
J: We'd forgotten how to do it.
Tom: We asked Simon.
Teacher: Did he know?
Tom: Yes.
Teacher: Show me how you measured with the protractor, Tom.

Tom demonstrates

Teacher: Has he got it right?

Others: Yes.

Teacher: I'm impressed with how well you have set up this experiment.

So far the teacher has asked the children about what they did. Now he goes on to explore what they have achieved. He probes their certainty about their results, 'Are you sure that the truck goes faster on the 10 per cent slope?', 'How can you check?' He finishes by asking pupils questions like: 'how do you feel you've got on?' 'what would you do differently?' before discussing with them what they might need to do next, finally agreeing the next realistic and achievable targets.

Feedback strategies can take many forms. Here are some you might like to consider using:

- *Written comments:* These can be very powerful, especially if time is made to reinforce the points made; the comment needs to reflect on the learning and how the learning was accomplished. An important point is to make sure that the writing is legible and written in language that the pupils are familiar with.

- *Oral comments about meeting the learning objective:* These can be quick and effective, especially where clarification or examples are needed

- *Target-setting comments*, either written or oral, about the 'how' to achieve the learning, with future action indicated.

- *Shared class marking:* time set aside in class to mark work as a class. This allows everyone to share knowledge and understanding by explaining and giving examples from the pupils' own work, and spotting where there is a need to adjust the teaching by moving on or going over aspects.

- *Paired marking:* Teaching pupils to be critical friends can take time and effort but this can be worth it. Simple checking that answers are correct is a useful first step.

- *Self-marking:* Eventually pupils can become their own critics, but to start with, checking that the work is mainly correct is a useful step on this road.

- *Teacher marking during the task:* Instant feedback for achievement and effort with the chance to reinforce and clarify learning.

The role of teaching assistants in providing feedback is something that needs to be considered. Your shared understanding about the ways that learning can be monitored is one way to make sure that the time in class is found to provide pupils with the information they need.

Clear marking criteria and related, constructive feedback

Informing the pupil about how well they have done by giving a letter grade or mark out of ten or a percentage would have been a reasonable response to work submitted in the past. All these are summative responses. The message would be 'well done' or 'you need to do better'. If you had 'done well' you may not be aware of what it was that was successful. If a pupil needed to 'do better' their question might be: 'How?' or 'What is it that I need to do?' The comment did not address this. The answer to how you could improve lay elsewhere. Formative feedback is not like this. Giving constructive formative feedback carries the implication that there will be information available which helps you to improve your work. Before considering how this might be done, there are some issues to be considered which might be considered as barriers to effectiveness.

Figure 10.1 Script One

Compare the two marked scripts in Figures 10.1 and 10.2.
Script One is given a grade as shown. It also offers correct
spellings. This is something a pupil could learn from if they
address the spellings. A long time ago, pupils were expected to
write their corrections three times each. Today, they might be
asked to copy the correct spellings into a vocabulary book for
future use. This would be considered a formative activity. The
comment cannot be acted upon as it offers no action apart from
an implication to try harder. There are no indications, apart
from spelling, to indicate how improvement might take place.

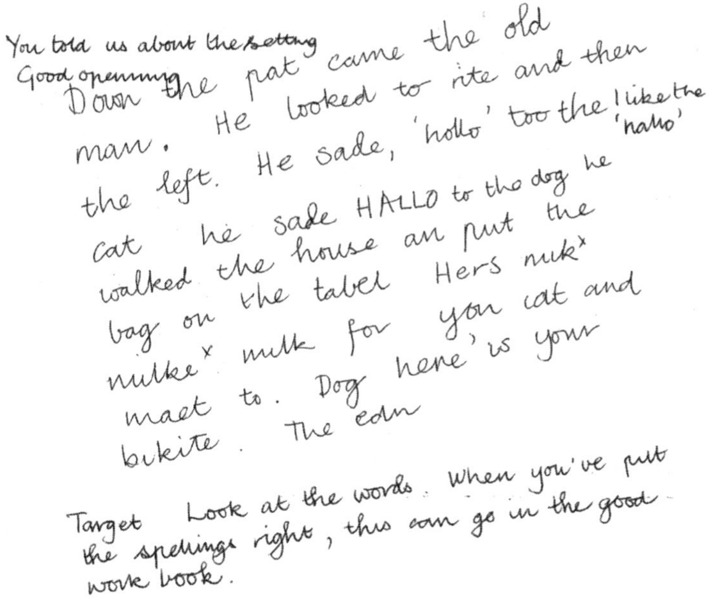

You told us about the setting
Good openning ~~the~~ pat came the old
Down the man. He looked to rite and then
the left. He sade, 'hollo' too the !like the 'hallo'
cat he sade HALLO to the dog he
walked the house an put the
bag on the tabel Hers ~~nuk~~ milk*
~~nulke~~* milk for you cat and
maet to. Dog here' is your
bikite. The edn

Target Look at the words. When you've put
the spelings* right, this can go in the good
work book.

Figure 10.2 Script Two

In Script Two there is a different approach. There is praise
for achievement and suggestion for improvement. The comment
at the bottom of the script offers a way forward. It is a more
constructive form of marking and there is an expectation that
the pupil will respond. As the teacher hands the work back he
says 'I really liked your first sentence. Think about the target I've
suggested.'

Neither of these will be effective in a formative way unless
the pupil is given time to respond. Handing the work back,
closing the book and moving on to the next piece of work will
break the formative cycle. Time must be given to enable the
pupil to read the comments and decide what action he or she
needs to take. If there is a misunderstanding, then this is the time
to sort it out. If there has been success then this needs to be

reinforced. When work is handed back, a strategy is needed to integrate the feedback into learning. How might this be achieved? (See Chapter 8 for some ideas about this.)

Homework plays a significant part in marked work. The same considerations should be given to comments made and time given to respond. It is particularly useful if the homework is linked to the objectives being met in the lessons. If this is done, then pupils should be clear about the objectives they need to achieve and, as well, how they might achieve them. It is important to do this as the 'how' is often the source of friction when pupils seek help at home.

Feedback in the form of grades

Interesting work is emerging which indicates that awarding grades overrides the comments made on a piece of work. This idea comes from Butler's (1988) controlled experiments where she had three conditions: grade only, comments only and grade plus comment. Her results surprised many teachers. She found that comments only were very effective in raising performance. Of course, the comment in the experiment followed best practice ideas on formative feedback. They were not the brief, 'Say more', 'Explain' notations in the margin that pupils can, and often do, choose to ignore. Grades alone just seem to confirm to pupils that they can or cannot do the subject: 'I can't do sums and my marks are always poor.' As Clarke (2003, p.9) puts it: 'Unfortunately, children quickly decide that they lack ability when constantly compared to other children in the class by explicit or implicit means or when their particular strengths are not valued.' Grades plus comments mean that they seem only to take account of the grades and the comment is overlooked. This feels counter-intuitive. Instinctively you would think that both would be better. But no, the comment on its own, especially where it relates directly to the marking criteria, and when time is allowed for reflection, seems to allow pupils most chance of learning.

Action plans and target setting

Already referred to is the teacher's evaluation of the lesson and the recognition of the need to review, consolidate or move on. Action can also be part of the expectation of individual pupils. In considering the feedback that pupils receive, it is important to consider whether any part of the action is longer term and could be a target for improvement. (See target setting in Chapter 11.)

Creating pupils who can self-assess through pupil strategies

So far in this chapter we have only mentioned feedback and target setting that has been entirely initiated by the teacher. If everything is controlled by the teacher, how will pupils learn to understand their own learning? Is it worth considering if pupil self-assessment is part of your own teaching model? Getting children to reflect on their own learning and deciding on action is a powerful model and does much to move children towards independent learning. For effective pupil self-evaluation to take place there needs to be time for it to take place and pupils themselves need to understand the process. You can promote self-assessment skills within lessons and as part of the feedback process. Self-assessment and evaluation can support and increase engagement with learning. Children who become used to this approach are more likely to make suggestions about how to progress their own learning.

Knowing what you know is a powerful tool. Tom worked out 'winning' when reading aloud by looking and thinking hard. He said: 'win', then looked at the teaching assistant and said, pointing, 'is that bit "ing"?' When she nodded, he said 'win-ning'. Having had a minimum amount of support, Tom is now better placed to make judgements about reading new words for himself. Crucially, he will become more independent in more areas of his work. Success in his reading may make him braver in other subjects. What is happening is that the child is learning to 'talk about learning in his head' or 'thinking about thinking'. Metacognition, knowing what you know, and making judgements about what to do to learn, is clearly a tool used by confident and self-evaluating learners. Because this involves ipsative assessment, it is building on previous learning so the targets will be realistic. Tom, when asked if he can read the next pages for himself, will use his knowledge about himself as a reader to judge whether the target is realistic. If he is successful, then he will make a judgement and be able to say to his teacher: 'I can read the rest of this story, for myself.' And if he is successful in meeting that target, then the climate is set for more self-assessment and target setting.

The questions that we need to get pupils asking are:

- What do I want to improve or what do I need to change?

- What can I try out?

- Did it work?

You will have noticed that the target setting described is very low-key. These are moment by moment opportunities to celebrate tiny amounts of learning. Building one word successfully encourages the child to try more word-building; reading to the end of the page means he or she will try reading to the end of the story. Very soon this confidence will mean that this child thinks of him or herself as a reader. Even if there is still some way to go in mastering all the things that need to be in place to actually read, this step, thinking of oneself as a competent reader, is important.

There is another sort of target setting. This is rather grander. Some school reports have a space for targets to be identified. These targets are shared with parents and carers. They can have time limits attached to them. The problem with school reports is that they are usually issued towards the end of the year so that targets attached to them may not be carried over into the next class. The next teacher will need to know that targets have been set and what these are. It is possible for this aspect of the information passed between classes and schools to be missed. If that happens, then it is a lost opportunity. The celebration of targets achieved has got to be seen as important. Targets once a year or even once a term seem very long-term; it is tempting to put off addressing them until another day. It seems appropriate to have targets that are short-term and manageable, small steps than can be soon achieved.

Often targets are set by teachers from the evaluation of a pupil's work or behaviour. The teacher is the prime decision-maker and the pupils' agreement may be sought, but usually with the expectation that they are going to agree. This gives the impression that the pupil has little say in the target setting. Only a slight change in approach is needed to make target setting pupil-centred. A key part of target setting is the way the target is going to be achieved. Tom sets himself a little more reading each day; his target reads: 'to finish the story by the end of the week'. A pupil decides that she is fed up with her teacher, her friends and her Mum moaning about her poor handwriting. Her self-set target is 'to improve my handwriting by half term'. Her approach is 'to practise for five minutes each day' and her success criterion is for her friend to be able to read her work. Her Mum helps by buying some new and fancy pens. Her teacher helps by providing letter-formation, letter-joining and other practice cards, and then assists by making the target a reality by doing things such as suggesting where to start a letter, checking writing position and by making sure that the time is available. These and other specific strategies make the target achievable. These teaching duties take very little time and this would seem to be time well spent.

If goals are shared, then some time should be given to addressing targets in school. It raises a picture in which, because targets are about individual needs, every child may be working on something different, for at least some part of the day or the week. Not an image we currently witness very often in school! Where this happens the child has to be very clear about how the work relates to the target, what strategies will be needed and how to measure success. The question for the teacher is how to support this through skilful use of the teacher's and the teaching assistant's time. Co-workers, the teaching assistants, are an essential part of this agenda. Their detailed knowledge about the individual pupils is hard to beat. Often their judgement about strategies is extremely helpful in making targets achievable. Pupil–pupil support will be part of this equation. Tom, with his new confidence as a reader, will gain from helping another child read the story he has just finished. Older pupils can support younger children, pupil helpers from the secondary school and parents all become part of the teacher's workforce when addressing individual's targets.

What is the balance between target work carried out in school and at home? In the handwriting target some thought was given to this. The child concerned decided for herself that if left entirely to home it might not happen at all. It takes time to explain to the people at home what the strategies for achieving the target are. Handwriting practice at home seems straightforward but in letter formation the direction of the stroke is important. If the kinaesthetic pattern is learned incorrectly then it can make for more problems. The letter formation was learned and checked in class. Only when the child and the teacher were confident that this was correct did it become homework. If this is not done then the target might be interpreted at home in ways which had not been anticipated. If it is the only work to go home it might receive more input than you were anticipating and become 'a big thing' of which the pupil becomes weary. Handwriting practice might become something the child worries about and which raises tension between child and Mum which is not helpful for the child, parent or the teacher. Homework should be a positive experience for all parties. If target work becomes homework then a clear understanding about the task must exist for all concerned.

Targets can be set for groups of children, whole classes, whole year groups and occasionally whole schools. Target setting includes strategies for achievement and success criteria.

A real example of a whole-school target setting

> All the children were set the target of saying 'please' and 'thank you' to the servers at lunchtime. How they might do this was discussed in small groups in class time. One class worked out how to achieve the target as a drama activity, eventually performing for the whole school. Another class made posters. Other classes did other activities. The servers were asked to tally every 'please' and 'thank you' on two days, randomly each week. This tally was shared with all the children. Very soon, long before the half-term set for its achievement, the children were thanked by the servers for the increase in what they termed 'old-fashioned good manners'. You can imagine that most of the children involved in this felt great. Incidentally from this small step, the school staff were able to begin to make good citizenship a feature for which they got very good reports in their next Ofsted report.

Assessment and evaluation

The terms assessment and evaluation are so closely linked it is sometimes difficult to identify the difference. Whereas assessment carries the implication that there is evidence which will speak for itself, the word evaluation implies that a judgement is being made about the situation or evidence collected. And yet, in both summative and formative assessment, a judgement is made. In summative assessment a grade given or a comment recorded is a form of judgement. In formative assessment a decision will be made and action will be taken. In evaluation a judgement is made as a result of which there is often an intention that future action will be taken. This makes it impossible to separate the two. If formative assessment and evaluation are both viewed as a process then the model is almost identical. An objective is set and carried out, evidence is collected of success, a decision is made and a new objective set. Such a process is a powerful mechanism for improvement and for learning.

Pupil self-evaluation

Consideration has been given to the formative process of assessment but now it is appropriate to link this process to what is generally known as self-evaluation. As trainees and teachers, we are always seeking to be more effective in our teaching and ensure effective learning takes place with our pupils. This is done by refining our teaching skills and matching the learning environment as closely as possible to the learners' needs. There are things to look for in the planning, the teaching and the pupils' responses which will indicate strengths and weaknesses and provide targets to enhance our effectiveness.

The logical parallels to self-evaluation of your own teaching skills are to apply the same processes to working with children. All the same arguments apply. If evaluation and action lead to improvement, progress should be possible in developing effective learning with children. Many teachers keep records where they place information about individuals. There is a strong case to make for these records being more proactive and formative. If the evaluation process is used by individuals this would provide a strong model of assessment for learning of an ipsative nature.

By using the evaluation/assessment process on their own learning, pupils can generate a model which carries the development of their learning forward. To do this they need to identify a target for improvement. They then decide, maybe with the assistance of the teacher, on a strategy to deal with the situation. It is no good a pupil saying, 'I want to improve my maths so I will try harder'. Pupils need to identify an action that they can take such as 'I'll find out how to work out the area of a triangle'. They then need to keep to the plan. After a suitable trial they assess whether their strategy was effective and can be used again. If the answer is 'yes', keep the strategy. If the answer is 'no', then try a different action. In this way they will gradually build a repertoire of successful learning. The process of self-evaluation is cyclic and has several stages. The stages for the pupil are the same as those for teachers developing their professional skills:

1. Identify the cause for concern.
2. Consider the available strategies.
3. Select a strategy.
4. Consistently use the strategy.
5. Evaluate its effectiveness.
6. If yes, keep it in the repertoire.
7. If no, select another strategy and try again.
8. Identify a new concern.

The cycle needs to be taught and may include a structure similar to the one below:

1. *Identify the cause for your concern*
Either something is not going well or you want to strengthen a situation or you want to learn something new. Identify what you want to change. It might be a problem such as spelling or hand-writing. Sometimes the cause is less obvious; in this instance the pupil needs to know to seek the help of the teacher to identify it.

2. *Consider the available strategies*
Once you have identified the problem or object of change you need to select a strategy. For example, to improve handwriting you could do some written exercises. Once again the advice will be to talk to the teacher as he or she will offer a way forward. Other advice will include: 'ask someone in your class who is good at . . .' This way they learn that sometimes it is helpful to consult classmates as they might have worked through or be working through the same issues and can offer mutual support.

The rest of the cycle as prepared for pupils might read like this:

3. *Select a strategy*

Select the strategy which you think will be most effective in your situation. You may wish to select more than one strategy and trial them simultaneously.

4. *Try it out*

Having decided what you are going to do, try it. You may decide to trial your chosen strategy over one day or several days.

5. *Did it work?*

It is important to evaluate the effectiveness of what you chose to do. This is an important part of the process. By returning to ask whether the strategy worked or not is part of the conscious process of permanently adopting the strategy or rejecting it. Don't expect all your strategies to be successful. Some must just be thrown out whilst others can be modified and given another go.

6. *If yes, keep it in the repertoire*

If the strategy worked then give yourself a pat on the back and make sure you keep using it for as long as it is appropriate.

7. *If no, select another strategy and try again*

Not everything is going to work first time. If the strategy does not work it is worth talking to someone about the problem. They might have a different view of the cause and can help you think it through. It might be that you have selected an appropriate strategy but it is going to take time to work. Try selecting another strategy. Now you have thought and observed more about the problem you might decide that a different strategy is more appropriate.

8. *On to the next strategy*

If you have been successful you will be ready to work on another problem so move on to your next target. If success has eluded you, have a rethink and persevere with the same strategy or select a new one. It is important to sustain the momentum and make the evaluative process part of your normal learning.

Self-evaluation is a powerful process. We are recommending you use it with your pupils. This can generate a challenging professional environment where you recognize there are many needs to be met and not enough time to meet them all. This is not a happy thought, but responding to individual needs will bring about more effective learning, so you have a responsibility to manage how time is spent. Part of the solution lies in getting children to be more independent in their learning and getting them to work with each other so that they can go some way to meeting their own needs. This implies that the classroom becomes more a learning community than a totally teacher-led experience.

Summary

The use of constructive feedback has implications for the management of time in classrooms. Because teachers will need to be available to individuals, pupils have to become more self-reliant. Part of this is to do with establishing classroom routines. Many minute-by-minute decisions that can take all a teacher's time need to be in the pupil's control: they need to know what to do if their pencil leads break, if they need more paper, which work has to be done in which book, which work has to be done, which work is an extension activity, and so on. Part of it is to do with careful planning with co-workers and part of it is to do with the role you expect pupils to take. Teaching assistants have time that needs to be used effectively. Other adults, pupils from your own school or from the next school up can all be part of the equation. As formative feedback becomes established it is likely that many pupils will become more reflective and aware of their successes and know more about their own learning processes. This self-knowledge will give them increased confidence to know and express their views about how and what they learn. It is about recognizing that everyone learns the same things but not necessarily in the same way. Through self-evaluation issues are sorted out and become part of the teaching routines.

11 Record keeping

Introduction

Record keeping can have at least three main purposes:

- to track the educational progress of the pupils in the class and prompt you for future action;

- to provide evidence for reporting progress to others;

- for pupils to track their own progress and take action.

For many teachers records are seen as an additional task which has to be done at intervals to indicate what children have covered in lessons. Records should be used in a much more proactive way to inform planning and action from day to day as well as to summarize progress.

Informal record keeping

Informal records are a form of aide-memoire, a note to yourself about the learning that is or is not taking place within the lesson. Some teachers like to make notes as the lesson progresses; others note down significant points at the end of the lesson or at the end of the day. When marking, more notes may be made about the pupils' learning. All these informal notes are there to support your evaluation of children's learning. The evaluation will probably centre on the following three questions:

- Do they know that well enough to move on?

- Do they understand but need another visit to consolidate their learning?

- Do they need to go back and begin again or sort out a misconception?

This will then feed into the next lesson planning. Some of the information will be transferred to more formal records. This transfer might occur at the end of one lesson or at the end of a series of lessons.

Recording against learning objectives or learning outcomes is an informal level of record keeping and serves the purpose of keeping track of individual learning. This informal record keeping will underpin more formal records that teachers are required to make. As we have already explained, in the National Numeracy Strategy (DfES, 1999) it is recommended that teachers record individual progress against the key objectives and that this is passed on to the next teacher. The teacher will also be able to use informal records to spot patterns of achievement and needs, which in turn will feed into individual pupil's short-term targets. Some teachers choose to record the barriers to learning, i.e. difficulties rather than the successes, because it is these points that they are going to act upon. Some teachers like to record significant incidents. Some collect work which shows significant development. This can be kept in a folder which is used to build a profile of a child.

When there is more than one adult working in the classroom, it could be that both are collecting assessment data. The teacher will need to plan what she or he wants the other adult to observe, what should be recorded and make time to share planning and outcomes. In all settings good communication is vital. This is especially so in Foundation Stage where there are often several adults working together.

The way data are collected varies. In some schools staff use a strategy where each adult collects data about particular pupils.

Table 11.1 Group record sheet 1

Group focus	Objective **To count to 20** **To recognize numerals to 20**	Date **30/6/05**
Name	**Response**	**Future action**
Warren	Counts to 20, muddles numerals 14 and 15	14 and 15
Angie	Counts to 30, knows all numerals	Counting in 10s
Pat	Counts to 12	Teen numbers
Jamisha	Counts to 20, knows all numerals	Counting in 10s
Micky	Counts to 20, muddles numerals 16 and 17	16 and 17
Jarred	Counts to 20, muddles numerals 16, 17 and 19	16, 17, 19

In other schools data collection is organized around the activity, the task and everyone feeds information into the informal records depending on which children they are worked with. In early years' settings, information can be collected about a learning objective but is just as likely to be about the achievements the children display, whatever the theme of the session. At the end of the week there is often a meeting where individuals and their needs are discussed.

Table 11.1 is an example of a group record sheet. This may be used when you are working with a group or you are observing and assessing a particular selection of pupils. The future action section offers targets to which it may be possible to respond in the next lesson or at some other convenient time.

Table 11.2 is another example of a group record sheet. This is

Table 11.2 Group record sheet 2

Subject area	Assessment/observation		
Teacher/Support	Class		Date
Objective	✓	understood/voluntary response	
	/	understood with further direction	
	✗	needs further experience/ inappropriate response	
	S	full support needed	
	A	audible response	
	R/e	responded with expression	
	I	involved in session	
	D	distracted easily	

Activity

Name	Observation/ assessment notes	Can explain/ add detail	Able to answer with relevance and confidence	Progression

one used by Owler Brook Nursery and Infant School, Sheffield. Note how it could be used as part of the evaluation of learning or as an unsupported assessment. Also note that it is being used by other adults in the classroom, not just the teacher.

The class record in Table 11.3 allows you to view the whole class at a glance. It shows which pupils need further attention. It is useful when marking work and assists planning the next session. It is also useful for review of individuals' progress in any one subject.

Table 11.3 Class record sheet

Maths 5B Objective Name	Can measure area counting squares	Can use rounding method on irregular shapes	Can find area of rectangle	Knows rule area of triangle

Table 11.4 Individual record sheet

Name	Teacher/Support	Date

Focus of assessment:

Task	Response

Records where a sheet is used for an individual are either part of an ongoing record or they are being used in a detailed observational way. Maybe there is a concern and a diagnostic record needs to be made (see Table 11.4).

So far, reference has been made to learning outcomes but teachers record other things which are part of educational development. When monitoring a child whose behaviour is a barrier to learning, a log may be kept on 'catching the child being good', as well as misdemeanours, any goals set for the pupil to work on and the strategies the teacher has used to modify behaviour. It is important to be clear about the assessment criteria. If you are collecting data about learning, unless behaviour is the prime cause for not learning, do not record information about it. If it is a prime concern then it is appropriate to note the action that needs to be taken, like in the next science lesson pairing a pupil with a different pupil, i.e. one likely to have a positive effect. What is a carried forward to the progress/achievement records is the information about what has or has not been learned, not the conduct.

Another aspect which teachers consider worth recording is pupils' attitude to work in different subjects and their ability to work as part of a group. When tracked in nursery, a very able child avoided all the artistic, creative activities because he was not so successful at them. Tracking highlighted this pattern, and consequentially the teacher began to use strategies to encourage and involve him in more creative tasks.

Using ICT to record

There are many packages being promoted by publishers and software companies which offer systems that you can use to record pupil performance. In England, these are usually linked to the National Curriculum or the Strategies. LEAs have an interest in collecting data too and the DfES has launched an electronic system to do this. It is called PAT and is referred to later in this chapter.

All paper and electronic records in public organizations are subject to the Data Protection Act (1998) which means that an individual can ask to see them. This includes school records, class records and even emails. This is a good and sufficient reason to keep to yourself personal comments based on opinion. It is a sound rule only to record what you can provide evidence for. Your professional judgements are entirely appropriate when they are based on evidence, either recorded – i.e. a child's work – or from observations.

Recording for classroom management

This form of recording is an organizational aid. It is about: Who has finished the work? Who missed science? Which group needs to do that task? Who hasn't used the computer yet? These are all things the teacher needs to track to ensure an equable curriculum but they are not about what a pupil has learned. Some teachers run a combined record sheet on opportunity and achievement. As long as you make sure you are recording achievement in learning, it is up to you (see Table 11.5).

Table 11.5 Class management (tracker of completed work/difficulties)

Tuesday 12 April	Completed art (grasses)	Computer: (spirals)	Revisit 'ch'
Ahmed	✓	✓	
Belinda	pm	Partner?	Needs 1to1
Courtney	absent	absent	✓
David	pm	✓	
Eddie	✓	✓	Needs 1to1
Fatima	Hall display	Friday?	
Gina	pm	Part Belinda	

Records are not a guarantee of secured pupil knowledge

When pupils sit an exam the current state of their knowledge is measured in specific topics. This is like taking a snapshot and capturing a moment in time. The exam captures a state of knowledge in a pupil's brain at that particular time. Often this is dependent on a good memory and the ability to recall information under pressure. Ongoing record keeping sets out to note when a learning objective has been met. Realistically, this is only indicating that at the time when the topic was addressed the pupil showed an ability to engage with the subject. This is no guarantee that the pupil will remember it or be able to transfer the information to a new situation.

In a small-scale experiment where a careful class record was kept of the work covered and achieved by pupils in mathematics and the work that pupils spontaneously applied to a new situation, more often than not the second situation was a whole National Curriculum level below the current work being done by the pupils in the class. The fact that the knowledge was spontaneous was a good indication that this was knowledge which was secure, was being transferred and in a useable form. The message here is that records can be kept but we must be clear that they indicate immediate understanding and not necessarily long-term understanding or availability for transfer.

Much learning appears to have the quality of retrospective assimilation. A good visual example of this is someone learning to juggle. Before mastering this skill with two balls, whilst still struggling to keep two balls moving in the air, he or she goes on to try with three balls. At this point juggling with three balls is also unsuccessful but, and this seems strange, on returning to juggle with two balls he or she finds that this is now successful. What is happening here? Is it a time factor of assimilation or is it that doing something more challenging unlocks the door to the simpler task? If the answer to either of these questions is 'yes', this has implications for the difficulty of the learning objectives teachers set their pupils and on the nature of the records kept on their immediate achievement. Bruner's (1966) theory of the effectiveness of a spiral curriculum does provide for a return to the topics at intervals rather than a 'one-shot' approach. This would fit with this feature of learning. It also has implications for the level of challenge you offer your pupils and at what point or even whether you are prepared to move them out of their 'comfort zone'.

Records for others – reporting

Each year schools in England and Wales are required to report to parents. The school must report on the National Curriculum subjects and any national tests – currently the Key Stages 1, 2 and 3, SATs and GCSEs. Assessments are made at the age of five and are fed into the Foundation Stage Profile, to which parents and carers contribute. Levels of performance are reported to parents and the LEA. Parents may request a meeting to discuss their child's performance. These are not national tests as such but form a benchmark, the content of which can vary from region to region.

In advice to supply teachers, this summarizes the DfES advice about keeping records:

The introduction of the NC and the statutory reporting requirements have resulted in the need for all teachers to keep up-to-date and accurate records of pupils' performance. Schools are required to keep records on every pupil, including information on academic achievement, other skills and abilities and progress made in school. Records must be updated at least once a year. There are no requirements about how, or in what form records should be kept. Decisions about how to mark work and record progress are professional matters for schools. As a supply teacher it is important that you obtain the

school's/department's marking and record-keeping policies. You will also need to find out what the department's policy is on retention of evidence of pupil progress. Although it is not a statutory requirement, many schools now expect teachers to record a level for their pupils at the end of each year; some do so termly and others half-termly.
(www.teachernet.gov.uk/supplyteachers/)

As the advice above reminds us, school staff can choose the style of their report. Some elect the checklist approach, while others choose boxes in which to write a few lines. We might speculate that probably teachers prefer to tick the boxes, whilst parents prefer to get written reports. Parents may feel that the written words tell them more about their child's performance. They will also recognize that information on level of performance is very clear on the tick box form. In general teachers find the tick box quicker and, therefore, less onerous (see Tables 11.6 and 11.7).

Most schools additionally have parents' and carers' meetings where oral reports on progress are given. These can be in many forms. The most common is probably the individual interview by appointment. These might last five to ten minutes. Any unresolved issues will require a further appointment. At such events there is usually a chance for parents to see the work their child has done in the preceding weeks.

Another form of parents' meeting is when the children are present at the interview. This can be an interesting and effective dynamic. There is little room for manipulation when everyone is present! If the teacher makes sure the conversation is inclusive, this can be a very effective approach.

A third approach is to have an 'open' event. This can be especially effective towards the end of the year when children have skills to demonstrate and products to display. It is empowering for the child to be the guide to the school. There is not the time for private interview but these can be arranged as required.

Table 11.6 Annual Report to Parents/Carers – written comments

School

Name	Class	Date

National Test Results

English	Mathematics	Science

English

Mathematics

Science

Foundation Subjects

Religious Education

Class teacher comment

Head teacher comment

Parent/Guardian response

Table 11.7 Annual Report to Parents/Carers – a checklist report

National Curriculum Progress	Reception		
1. With the teacher's help 2. Beginning to understand 3. Understands well			
Speaking and listening	1	2	3
Listens well to adults and other children			
Listens to stories			
Speaks clearly to others			
Describes stories and events in detail			
Reading			

These events often have a sense of shared achievement and children and parents can be found visiting several of the classrooms, including those in which their children might find themselves in the following term.

When children first enter a new school, a meeting is often arranged early in the first term as an opportunity for parents and carers to check that their child has settled in. Some very successful schemes run where the reception teacher visits the child in their home environment before entering the school. This helps the child to see the link between home and school, it allows him or her to show the teacher some of their toys. The teacher is able to talk to the parents and begin to understand the child's home. This information will inform the way the teacher responds to the child in school.

As well as reporting to parents and carers, teachers are asked to write a report as part of assessments where children are identified as having barriers to learning. These reports are for the Special Needs Co-ordinator (SENCO), a member of school staff, support staff from the local authority, and other professionals, such as social workers and educational psychologists. These reports are often produced through the use of software which guides you through the sorts of data that will be used to form an opinion about appropriate action for a particular child in your class. In addition to your written report, it is likely that you will be part of the consultation process, so you will be expected to take part in case meetings that also inform decision-making.

As well as all this every child has a formal record that travels with them through his or her schooling. Teachers are expected to provide written information to be put in into this. To return to the National Numeracy Strategy (DfES, 1999), which we have used before, for maths, the DfES suggest that records of key objectives are passed on. Key objective numeracy record sheets can be found at www.standards.dfes.gov.uk/numeracy/publications/resources/. There is similar advice for Literacy on the Standards site as well.

Transfer from one class to another will usually require written and oral information to be passed on to the next teacher. There is considerable variation in practice about this, particularly so when a pupil is changing schools. School staff who do this well are those who have built a reputation for keeping records that provide a true reflection of children's achievements and attributes. These teachers are respected by their colleagues who rely on the records about the children they are receiving.

For national testing purposes and to identify local trends pupil performance information is also passed on to the LEA. As mentioned above, the DfES launched its Pupils Achievement Tracker (PAT) on 1 April 2005. These are some of the things that are claimed for it:

The Pupil Achievement Tracker (PAT) is a powerful piece of diagnostic and analytical software all school staff will want to use. Teachers can use it to ask questions about the effectiveness of their classroom practice looking at graphical data on the progress made by their pupils; set pupil targets informed by the progress made by similar pupils nationally; and understand fully what pupils can achieve by the diagnostic analysis of test papers.

Headteachers and senior managers can view recent performance against other similar schools to help set development priorities; ask questions about the achievement of different groups within the school; and review the success of different initiatives, particularly through the ability to group pupils and look at their achievement and progress.

The Pupil Achievement Tracker includes all the national data and brings it to life on screen, but takes it into the classroom by adding:

Pupil target setting, allowing schools to set targets informed by the progress made by similar pupils nationally. Using the PAT, each teacher will be able to view on screen the prior attainment of their current pupils. They will also see on screen possible targets for each child based on the recent progress made by pupils similar to theirs, taking account of their prior attainment. They will then decide what targets to set for each pupil, before reviewing the impact these targets will have on the overall progress made by pupils in their school. The school will be able to look at the implications for its overall targets and ensure that they reflect their aspirations for improvement in performance.

Question level analysis, bringing to life what pupils can achieve in National Curriculum and Optional Tests from Years 2 through to 9. The PAT fully incorporates the functionality of the 2003 QCA diagnostic software.

Analysis of value-added data by different cohorts within the school, including the ability to create groups of pupils. (www.standards.dfes.gov.uk/performance/)

Clearly these are big claims. It will be interesting to see how this innovation works out in practice.

A word of warning

It is very easy to systematically observe and record learning objectives and fragments of learning objectives and assume that a pupil is progressing. It might be that the pupil performs well in the short term but, over time, forgets knowledge and skills. A pupil might have the capacity for learning direct pieces of information but may not be able to assimilate it into the rest of his learning. Consequently he finds it difficult to apply learning to new situations. He is not able to make sense of new situations. It is as though he, and many other pupils, are unable to construct 'the bigger picture'. As Torrance and Pryor (1998) point out this is because assessments often measure fragmented limited task achievement. They remind us that to assess general understanding and capability is more useful and longer lasting. What this suggests is that it is important to step back from the bits of daily learning in order to get a sense of what is happening overall for each pupil. You can do this by asking yourself where you are heading with each of your pupils. There is definitely a need to view the holistic as well as the specific progress of each pupil in your class.

Additionally, Torrance and Pryor (1998, p.15) drawing upon the work of others (Wertsch, 1985, Shepard, 1991, Berlak *et al.*, 1992, Gifford and O'Connor, 1992) make the point that learning is not a staged move from the simple to the complex, but it is more about active engagement with what pupils encounter and incorporate into their developing scheme. This beautifully describes approaches to learning in the early years of education and makes us wonder why such an approach is sometimes lost as children progress through the primary school.

Profiles

A profile is a collection of information. The first question to ask yourself is: 'What is the purpose of keeping a profile?' This will govern decisions about what is put in it. You need to ask whether it is a depository of information or a proactive 'log'. The second question is: 'Who has ownership, the teacher or the pupil?' Here are some examples of profile types.

A profile of best work

This is often a folder for each pupil in which good-quality work is filed. This is a profile which celebrates achievement. It can be used to compile a summative report. It is likely that the work which goes into the profile will be pieces which you negotiate with the pupil: 'Shall we put this piece in? Or is this one better?' As it is something which pupils will be proud of it could be that the profile is taken home at the end of the year. However, some school staff will prefer to retain best-work profiles in school, using them with children at review points. Look upon this as an evidence-based record of achievement.

A profile of pupil progress

This type of profile is managed by the teacher. It is a record of a pupil's achievements. It is focused on the learning that has taken place. It will include a systematic record of achievement against curriculum objectives. It will also include success in meeting individual targets. This is much more a record of progress. It can also be used to comment and set targets on behaviour, engagement with work, social and academic skills. Angie might be very shy. To help her overcome this you decide to try out strategies to encourage greater communication and leadership of groups. The profile would be an appropriate place to record progress against your strategies.

Pupil ownership

You may choose to develop profiles which are owned and managed by the pupils themselves. In this kind of profile the pupils record their own progress and choose the work to exemplify their learning and successes. As the pupil moves up through the junior school, hybrid forms of this practice include a transition from the teacher-kept profile to the pupil-managed profile. This kind of profile is appropriate for pupils who are in charge of their own learning through identifying their own needs and setting targets to achieve them. They will probably need time and help with the 'how' but this is a strong move towards encouraging independent learning. It is also another way to develop ipsative assessment.

A shared profile

The following is an example of part of a shared profile used in Owler Brook Nursery and Infant School, Sheffield. The teacher records the pupil responses to the following statements on a folded A3 sheet:

My Evaluation

My name _____ Date _____

Our theme this term was _____

My best piece of work was _____

My favourite piece of work was _____

This term I have improved on _____

My own targets for next term are _____

Teacher's comment

Some aspects of the way the profile is created can be found in the case study: managing assessment in a Nursery Infant school at the end of Chapter 3.

The class teacher using records to support learning

Records can be used to inform teacher's decision-making over a longer time span. In Chapter 2 Peter was identified as not making expected progress during the teacher's routine assessment timetable. In weeks 4 and 5 she has a focus on the children's reading progress and, because it fits with the teaching activities, a close look at each child's phonic knowledge. What about the other children in Peter's class? At the end of this book it seems appropriate to think about the individuals who have barriers to learning and how formative assessment is used to identify and deal with these.

First, some background on the school which serves an area where housing is inexpensive to either rent or buy. This has attracted families from many countries, as well as white families on low incomes. The area is officially recognized as one where poverty is a real issue. One marker for this is the very high number of children who have free school meals. The school is newly built, bright and attractive, with a Nursery. Most families in the area choose to send their children to it. Many of the children have English as an additional language (EAL). The school has a high priority to ensure that children make good progress in English. This is achieved by ensuring that all classrooms have full-time classroom assistants, most of whom are bilingual and all of whom have strong links with the community. All the teaching staff have expertise in EAL. The curriculum and the teaching take account of this need. As you might expect there are also children who are refugees and asylum seekers. These children's additional needs for security and safety have also to be met through empathetic teaching. The whole staff team share the high aspirations for the children. The leadership of the Headteacher is an important factor in the school's success.

As they have now been in school from the age of four and half Peter's teacher has several useful ideas about each one of them. She uses the records that have been diligently kept to help with this. This is where having confidence in colleagues is important. The information supplied has to be reliable for it to be useful. In this instance the teacher has confidence in the records passed on to her. From these and her own observations and those of the classroom assistant she has a fairly clear idea about what each child knows and enjoys and how each one learns. There are thirty children in the class. Her own records, at this point in the year, shows that twenty-four children are making or exceeding progress expected. Of the remaining six children, two are very able, clever at their work and well ahead of most of the other children, the other four may be considered as pupils with special needs; they have barriers to learning that need to be addressed.

Children with special needs

In the procedures in schools in England there are three stages in recognizing children with special needs: registers are kept for children on School Action, School Action Plus and for those with Statements of Special Needs. The Special Needs Co-ordinator (SENCO) is the teacher in the school with special responsibilities for children with special needs. In this school she has her own class in the morning and works as SENCO in the afternoon. Initial decisions about children with barriers to learning are made with the children, their parents or carers, the class teacher and with the Special Needs Co-ordinator. In this school a systematic approach is used to assess children who may benefit from extra support. Each child has an Individual Education Plan (IEP) with clear learning objectives for each half term's work. Within the class as they work, the teacher and the classroom assistant keep a careful eye on their progress. The class teacher and the SENCO review children's progress regularly, informally every six weeks and formally twice each year. The SENCO assists the teachers by carrying out some one-to-one work to assess progress and makes suggestions for adjustment to the teaching programme. This is extra to the differentiation that each teacher expects to make to meet the needs of the range of children in the class.

Some children in the class were identified at age five as needing some additional help. Through the programme of regular review, in this class the teacher has, by this point in the year, moved five children, originally put into this category, off School Action list. The extra differentiation that was worked out to address their barrier to learning has enabled each to make sufficient progress to be a regular member of the class. Two children out of the four on School Action register are making the progress that is expected. Their barriers to learning are well understood and teaching is arranged to meet their needs. The teacher has identified the other two children who may benefit from further investigation. Both these children appear to be making much less progress in learning than might be expected. These two stand out when compared with the other children who are making progress. They always seem to take much longer to complete tasks and appear unsure about their learning. Ahmid, for whom English is second language, and Sarah-Louise are to be the focus of extra attention during the five weeks leading up to the next school holiday. This decision was made jointly by the teacher, the teaching assistant and the SENCO. To do this they use the record about the individual as evidence, supplementing this with whatever additional investigations are needed.

Ahmid's progress in English is not the focus of the teacher's concern. In this school the curriculum and assessment take account of the needs of EAL children. Bilingual support staff are used to enable children to work in their own language whilst they become fluent in English. The cause of concern is that Ahmid finds most learning hard. It is clear from the records about him that every assessment shows that his progress in his last year of infant school is very slow. While other children are moving on, Ahmid is struggling. The records also show that whenever he faces new situations he is slow to settle. This means that there is some concern that the move to the Junior school may create additional problems for Ahmid. The SENCO, as well as the teacher and teaching assistant are now of the opinion that Ahmid needs to be moved to School Action Plus. This will help the school pull in the resources to begin to identify and deal more fully with Ahmid's barriers to learning.

Sarah-Louise is not making much progress either, despite considerable effort by teaching staff. The records kept since she came to school support this view. Her reading and writing are more like that expected for a five year old. She does not do well at speaking and listening tasks. Her number work is also well below the standard expected for her age group. She has already progressed from School Action to School Action Plus. Now the parents, with school staff, are asking for additional investigation to see if she meets the criteria for a Statement of Special Needs. Again the reasons for asking for this investigation are to gain extra resources to enable Sarah-Louise to make progress.

The teacher and the teaching assistant in Peter's class place assessment at the centre of their teaching. The records from previous classes inform their opinions. However, it is the formative assessment of each pupil that helps them plan for individual progress; in turn this enables them to manage the class, sorting out groups and sorting out how, when and where the adults will spend their time.

Summary

Records serve a purpose. To make your record-keeping a functional part of your teaching you need to consider:

- What is the purpose for which you are keeping the record?

- What data would best inform you for that purpose?

- What is the best way to display that data?

- What will you do with the information you have collected?

- Who has ownership of the record?

There are many different audiences demanding the information you build up about your pupils. The most important audience is the pupils themselves.

Appendix   Dweck's theory

Dweck's (1989) theory helps us to understand children's inner needs. She takes learning goals and contrasts these with performance goals.

Children with learning goals	Children with performance goals
choose challenging tasks regardless of whether they think they have high or low ability relative to other children	avoid challenge when they have doubts about their ability compared with others
optimize their chances of success	tend to self-handicapping so that they have an excuse for failure
tend to have an 'incremental theory of intelligence'	tend to see ability as a stable entity
go more directly to generating possible strategies for mastering the task	concentrate much of the task analysis on gauging the difficulty of the task and calculating their chances of gaining favourable ability judgements
attribute difficulty to unstable factors, e.g. insufficient effort, even if they perceive themselves as having low ability	attribute difficulty to low ability
persist	give up in the face of difficulty
and remain 'relatively unaffected by failure in terms of self-esteem'	and become upset when faced with difficulty of failure

Dweck, 1989 p.111

Dweck recommends engaging in task analysis, adopting challenging standards based on personal progress and focusing on past and future success with effort and strategy the reasons for success or failure.

Reference

Dweck, C.S. (1989) 'Motivation', in A. Lesgold and R. Glaser (eds), *Foundation for Psychology of Education*, NJ: Laurence Erlbaum.

Further reading

Dweck, C.S. (1999a) 'Caution – praise can be dangerous', *American Educator* 23/1: 4–9.
Dweck, C.S. (1999b) *Self Theories: Their Role in Motivation, Personality and Development*, Philadelphia: Psychology Press.

References

Black, P. and Wiliam, D. (1998) *Inside the Black Box: Raising standards through classroom assessment*, London: School of Education, King's College.

Black, P., Harrison, C., Lee, C., Marshall, B. and Wiliam, D. (2003) *Assessment for Learning: Putting it into practice*, Maidenhead: Open University Press.

Bloom, B.S. (1956) *Taxonomy of Educational Objectives*, 2 vols, New York: Longman Green.

Boylan, M. (2004) 'Questioning (in) School Mathematics: Lifeworlds and Ecologies of Practice', PhD thesis, Sheffield Hallam University.

Brissenden, T. (1988) *Talking About Mathematics*, Oxford: Blackwell.

Bruner, J.S. (1966) *Towards a Theory of Instruction*, Cambridge, MA: Harvard University Press.

Butler, R. (1988) 'Enhancing and undermining intrinsic motivation: the effects of task-involving and ego-involving evaluation on interest and performance', *British Journal of Educational Psychology*, 58: 1–14.

Chaplian, R. (2000) 'Helping children to persevere and be well motivated', in D. Whithead (ed.), *The Psychology of Teaching and Learning in the Primary School*, London: Routledge.

Clarke, S. (2001) *Unlocking Formative Assessment*, London: Hodder and Stoughton.

Clarke, S. (2003) *Enriching Feedback in the Primary Classroom*, London: Hodder and Stoughton.

Cook, M. (2005) 'Collaboration, intervention and "third spaces": developing curriculum continuity between home and school', *Literacy* 39/2 (in press).

Dahlberg, G., Moss, P. and Pence, A. (1999) *Beyond Quality in Early Childhood Education: Postmodern Perspectives*, London: Routledge Falmer.

DfES (1999) *The National Numeracy Strategy*, DfES.

DfES (2000) *Mathematical Vocabulary Book*, DfES.

DfES (2000) *The National Curriculum*, DfES.

Dweck, C.S. (1989) 'Motivation', in A. Lesgold and R. Glaser (eds), *Foundation for Psychology of Education*, NJ: Laurence Erlbaum.

Dweck, C.S. (1999a) 'Caution – praise can be dangerous', *American Educator*, 23/1: 4–9.

Dweck, C.S. (1999b) *Self Theories: Their Role in Motivation, Personality and Development*, Philadelphia: Psychology Press.

Gipps, C. and Stobart, G. (1997) *Assessment: a teacher's guide to the issues*, London: Hodder and Stoughton.

Graham, L. and Johnson, A. with Bearne, E. (2003) *Children's Writing Journals*, Royston: United Kingdom Literacy Association.

Hall, K. and Burke, W.M. (2003) *Making Formative Assessment Work: Effective practice in the primary classroom*, Maidenhead: Open University Press.

Headington, R. (2003) *Monitoring, Assessment, Recording, Reporting and Accountability* (2nd edn), London: David Fulton.

Lepper, M. and Hodell, M. (1989) 'Intrinsic motivation in the classroom', in C. Ames and R. Ames (eds), *Research on Motivation in Education*, Vol 3: *Goals and Cognitions*, San Diego CA: Academic Press.

Nuttall, D. (1987) 'The validity of assessment', *European Journal of the Psychology of Education*, 11(2): 109–18.

Perrott, E. (1982) *A Practical Guide to Improving Your Teaching*, Harlow: Longman.

Porter, L. (2003) *Young Children's Behaviour*, London: Paul Chapman.

Rowe, M.B. (1974) 'Wait time and rewards as instructional variables, their influence on language, logic and fate control', *Journal of Research in Science Teaching*, 11: 81–94.

Sadler, R. (1989) 'Formative assessment and the design of instructional systems', *Instructional Science*, 18: 119–44.

Skemp, R. (1971) *The Psychology of Learning Mathematics*, Harmondsworth: Penguin.

Torrance, H. and Pryor, J. (1998) *Investigating Formative Assessment*, Maidenhead: Open University Press.

Watson, J.B. (1930) *Behaviourism*, New York: Norton.

Wertsch, J.V. (1985) *Vygotsky and the Social Formation of Mind*, Cambridge, MA: Harvard University Press.

Websites

www.assessment-reform-group.org.uk

www.nfer.ac.uk

www.qca.org.uk

www.standards.dfes.gov.uk

www.teachernet.gov.uk/